BUC E III

The Military History of Oxfordshire & Buckinghamshire

Edited by Stanley C. Jenkins. Design & layout Ian Pope.
ISBN: 9781899889396
© Lightmoor Press and the various contributors, 2009
Printed by The Information Press, Eynsham, Oxfordshire

Contents

EDITORIAL

When *Bugle & Sabre* was first conceived as an occasional publication containing material relating to the military history of Oxfordshire and Buckinghamshire, it was envisaged that the emphasis would be primarily on local history. However, when dealing with a regiment such as the Oxfordshire & Buckinghamshire Light Infantry, which served throughout the world, it soon became obvious that the subject matter of *Bugle & Sabre* would have to encompass locations far beyond the confines of England. Accordingly, this third edition contains three articles devoted exclusively to the United Kingdom, together with three contributions relating to the Boer War, The Western Front and Palestine.

Two of the articles in Bugle & Sabre III deal with controversial events – the Irish 'Troubles' of 1919-23 and the Jewish Revolt. There were, in many ways, similarities between these two episodes, both of which involved 'peace-keeping' duties in divided communities, although the situation in Ireland in 1919 was particularly difficult in that the Oxfordshire & Buckinghamshire Light Infantry found itself under attack in what was still regarded as an integral part of the British homeland.

In researching the Irish article, help was gratefully received from Pádraig Óg Ó Ruairc, an Irish historian who has carried out ground-breaking work in the Black & Tan campaign and the Irish Civil War. Indeed, there was a useful exchange of information between Pádraig and the Soldiers of Oxfordshire Trust to the extent that SOFO was able to provide some additional details for Pádraig's own book *The Blood On the Banner: the Republican Struggle in Clare*. Former members of the regiment may be interested to known that, in Pádraig's opinion, the Oxfordshire & Buckinghamshire Light Infantry maintained its good reputation during the Irish 'Troubles', insofar as it remained a well-disciplined regiment that did not, in general, take unnecessary 'reprisals' against the local population.

Stanley C. Jenkins, Witney, 2009

Cover: **A review of cadets at the Royal Military College, Great Marlow.**

A colour print depicting a review of gentlemen cadets of the Royal Military College at Great Marlow in 1810. From an original water colour in the possession of Major Coningsby Disraeli.

Oxfordshire & Buckinghamshire Light Infantry Museum OBLI5402

REMNANTZ 1718 - 2007
FAMILY HOME & MILITARY COLLEGE
Caroline Osborne

Remnantz, a large 18th century house in Marlow, Buckinghamshire, which had been established by the Remnants, a family of iron founders, was until recently the home of the Wethered family. The Wethereds were brewers of fine beer, local squires, magistrates and MPs, churchmen and professional soldiers and sailors. The Wethereds were, among others, founders of the Buckinghamshire Rifle Volunteers, which ultimately became the (Territorial) Buckinghamshire Battalion of the Oxfordshire & Buckinghamshire Light Infantry. Before it was purchased by the Wethered family, Remnantz was used as the first Royal Military College, where Gentleman Cadets were educated and trained for commissioning into the Regular Army.

This article was written by Caroline Osborne, née Wethered, using material collected by her brother Anthony for his book about the Wethereds, *The Power and the Brewery*. In addition to her own memories, she has recorded some of her brother Julian's who, with Caroline and Anthony, knew Remnantz as a family home.

ORIGINS & BACKGROUND

The house that we now know as 'Remnantz' takes its name from a previous owner, Stephen Remnant, who was a successful iron founder and government contractor from Woolwich. In 1750 he acquired property in Marlow and set about converting it into a gentleman's residence. We do not know for sure who designed and built the original Marlow house that Remnant acquired, but we do know that in 1718 a certain Stephen Peters, a merchant from London, began buying up parcels of land in the western part of Marlow which, when put together, were to make up the Remnantz property. Peters is on record as having paid £200 for 'a dwelling, a malt house, an orchard and an acre of pastureland'. It is thought that it was he who then built the severe looking box-like structure which still forms part of the house, dated by Pevsner as circa 1720.

Stephen Peter's wife Sarah was the widow of a Samuel Remnant who had died in the 1690s, by whom she had had one son, also called Samuel. She then had a daughter by Stephen Peters, called Mary, who married a local man from Bisham, called Samuel Manning. Manning bought land adjoining his father-in-law's house in Marlow, which he made into a walled kitchen garden. This remained in existence until 1995. When Stephen Peters died in 1738, his daughter Mary and son-in-law Samuel Manning inherited the property in law. They had a daughter called Sarah.

Meanwhile, Samuel Remnant (the younger) and his son Stephen had set up as partners in an iron foundry behind the gun wharf in Woolwich. By 1730, Samuel Remnant was in charge of the gun wharf foundry as well, and he and Stephen had become well-established suppliers to the Royal Ordnance. The foundry was adjacent to the Ordnance Depot on the site of an old rabbit warren. This was the 30-acre site on which guns were tested - and occasionally exploded. It was indeed called the 'Woolwich Warren' until 1805, when George III renamed it 'The Royal Arsenal'.

It is understood that Samuel the father was not entirely scrupulous in his dealings. In 1750 he successfully escaped legal action arising from an investigation of his dealings by the Surveyor General. Samuel died in 1752, within 18 months of the report being issued, but in the same year his son and erstwhile partner Stephen Remnant and his sister, Sarah Redwood, were forced to repay the Crown more than £10,000. Despite having had their fingers burned with Samuel Remnant, the Army continued to do business with Stephen - in 1761 he was to patent a 'skeleton' iron gun carriage, which became a model for carriages of that type.

Samuel Remnant is buried with his wife in Woolwich. The Remnant and Peters families had come together again in 1747 when Stephen, grandson of Samuel Remnant the elder, married his half cousin Sarah Manning, granddaughter of Stephen Peters.

It was about this time that Stephen Remnant acquired through the Mannings the property in Marlow he was to call Remnantz. He owned it for over half a century, and turned it into a fine residence. It was Stephen, we believe, who employed a famous architect, Sir Robert Taylor, to design the interior of the house with its beautiful pedimented door cases, marble fire places and the fine wooden staircase cantilevered to look like stone. The grand Venetian window overlooking the garden is attributed to Taylor and the very detailed plasterwork ceiling, which is a good example of the genre, with musical instruments, flags and weapons of war representing 'the arts of peace and war'. (It is remarkable that after many lettings, periods of neglect and ten years of the Army, and who knows how many coats of paint, that the plaster and other work is as well preserved as it is today).

Stephen and Sarah had four children, two sons and two daughters. Both daughters married into the Army, Captains Murray and Chapman, who both eventually became generals. We do not know how much time Stephen and Sarah or their childrens' families actually lived in Remnantz; it is believed that the house was let for some of the fifty years that Stephen was the owner.

We know that in 1799 Stephen Remnantz was living in Kent. Sarah had died in 1788 and Stephen is recorded as trying to let Remnantz. He died in 1801, and in his will directed that his executor and son in law, Richard Chapman sell the house. Chapman's daughter, who had married the son of a John Groves, persuaded Chapman to buy the Marlow property himself at auction for £2,061 10s, 'to save it from going out of the Remnant family'.

THE MILITARY COLLEGE

It happened that in 1801, the War Office was looking for temporary quarters to accommodate the junior branch of its newly formed Royal Military College, near the senior branch, which was being established in High Wycombe. The College was the brainchild of a remarkable officer from Guernsey, Colonel (later Major General) John Le Marchant of the Dragoon Guards. It was a bold scheme to provide officer cadets between the ages of 13 and 15 with a general education and to prepare them for military life.

Offered a lease by Richard Chapman, a rising star in the Army, the War Office looked favourably on Remnantz and its grounds in Marlow. A meeting at Horse Guards was attended by, among others, notably the Duke of York – the 'Grand Old Duke of York', who was the Commander-in-Chief – and the Secretary of State for War, a gentleman by the name of Charles Yorke, with an 'e'.

They approved an expenditure of £400 7s 11d for fitting the house out and a further £124 for 'building a chimney in one of the offices belonging to the said house'. They also approved the style of bedding to be used by the cadets. The College's 'Supreme Board' agreed an annual rent of £120 and the first batch of 16 cadets arrived in May 1802. As the numbers grew to over 400, several temporary buildings were erected in the grounds, and other properties in the town were also taken on.

There is written evidence that life for the Gentleman Cadets was fairly rigorous, each day starting with a parade and inspection at 6 am. At 6.30 am there were prayers followed by two hours of study. Breakfast was served at 9 am after which they studied from 10 am until 12 noon. Then came 'fencing, riding, swimming and the sabre'. Dinner was at 2 pm, then study until 5.30 pm, when there was an hour of military exercises. At 8.30 pm they had supper followed by prayers and 'the retreat' at 9 pm.

Each cadet was provided annually with:

- One scarlet infantry jacket, with blue cuffs and collar, looped with silver.
- One scarlet waistcoat, without sleeves.
- Two pair of blue pantaloons.
- One felt cap
- Two pairs short black gaiters
- Two or more pairs of shoes.

And in addition, '1 blue greatcoat' was provided every three years.

The teaching staff was high quality. It included a future Head Master of Bath Grammar School, a mathematics professor who was a member of the Royal Society, and a future Lady Margaret Professor of Divinity at Oxford. A brother of Thomas Arnold of Rugby also taught there. In the days before photography and Ordnance Survey maps, army officers had to be good draughtsmen. Maps, orders of battle, fortifications and the like had to be sketched in the field, and consequently there were several drawing masters on the staff; Le Marchant himself was a talented artist. The College even offered a place to John Constable, but he declined to take it on the advice of the President of the Royal Academy. He preferred haywains to unruly cadets! In 1808 the Army Commander-in-Chief, Frederick Duke of York, visited the College.

To the town of Marlow, the College was a mixed blessing; the young Gentleman Cadets were not always well behaved. They were known to throw stones at professors, insult women, owe money to shop keepers and behave in a drunken manner! And in 1804 the vigilance of guards foiled an attempted mutiny: the culprits were expelled and their swords were broken over their heads.

The junior branch of the Royal Military College was at Remnantz from 1802 until 1812. It then moved to Sandhurst. Sadly the founder of the College, General Le Marchant was not to see the Gentlemen Cadets move into their grand new purpose-built college – he was killed at the battle of Salamanca. Richard Chapman died a general in 1811. By then his daughter Jane-Sarah and John Thomas Groves had had a son, John Richard, who inherited the house. He was only twenty-two and a lieutenant in the Rifle Brigade. He might be forgiven for having thought it a mixed blessing and eventually in 1825 John Richard Groves, the great-grandson of Stephen and Sarah Remnant, sold the property for £2,000 to my great, great, great grandfather Thomas Wethered, a local brewer.

THE WETHEREDS AT REMNANTZ

Thomas Wethered, with his flourishing Brewery and large family was already well established in Marlow. In 1744 a George Wethered, who had come from Penn, married Elizabeth Gibbons, who was the daughter of a Marlow brewer and maltster. They had a son George. Elizabeth died and George senior married again and had another son called Thomas. When their father died, young George inherited the maltings and Thomas the brewery. But they quarrelled and took their quarrel to the High Court. Following the judgement George sold the maltings business and left Marlow for ever. The brewery however prospered. Thomas and his wife Sarah became great benefactors of the town; evidence of this remains on many of its public buildings.

The Wethereds knew a number of the officers and teachers on the College staff with whom they had shared quite a gay social life, going to parties and musical

A watercolour by Thomas Wethered's daughter Martha, based on an 1804 painting of Remnantz by T. Weston.

Caroline Osborne

evenings in each other's houses. (Thomas's eldest daughter fell hopelessly in love with the future Oxford Professor, Godfrey Faussett, but she was in her teens and he was ten years her senior and went off to marry another lady. However the families kept in touch and when Faussett's wife died, he came back and married Sarah!)

On purchasing Remnantz, Thomas Wethered promoted himself from 'brewer' to 'gentleman' in the local trade directory. He set about turning the house back into a home. He demolished the west wing and lowered the roof of the remaining L-shaped house, extended the middle section, making a 35-foot drawing room with bedrooms above. He added bow windows to both the front and garden sides. He and his wife, Sarah, had ten children, so the space was important. Thomas used the unwanted bricks from the demolished part of Remnantz to enlarge the brew house. The brewery was a short walk from Remnantz along a narrow alleyway.

Thomas Wethered died in 1849 and his heirs enjoyed living in his redesigned home for a further 158 years. The family brewery continued to provide for the family and the townsfolk of Marlow until it was sold to a major brewery company in 1949. Sadly, in 1998, after 240 years, it ceased to be a brewery. The buildings were demolished and the site redeveloped for housing. (When Thomas died in 1849, the brewery was producing about 200 barrels a week. When the brewery finally closed down in 1987, it was producing 1,800 barrels a week).

It was Thomas's grandson Owen Peel Wethered, aged twenty-two, who in 1858 acted on a letter from the Lord Lieutenant of Buckinghamshire, Lord Carrington, which suggested that Marlow provide a Corps of Volunteers to serve in the event of an attempted French invasion. In December 1859 Owen – known as 'OPW' - chaired an inaugural meeting in Marlow and signed up the first 33 members of the Bucks Rifle Volunteers. Owen enlisted

as a Private, served for over 30 years and ended up as their Honorary Colonel.

Owen Wethered recalled of the early days that 'the officers were mortally afraid of offending their men, many of whom were of equal social standing with themselves... My brother came to my home one evening on his way to drill and said: *"Look here, Owen, I notice that when I give the word 'Fall In', many of the men fall in with their pipes in their mouths. Now I'm sure that can't be right, so I want you to fall in tonight your pipe in your mouth. I shall then pitch into you, and after that I can blow up anyone else who does it"*. The ruse was duly carried out I was roundly pitched into and after that evening pipes were duly pocketed at the 'Fall In'.

In 1881 the Bucks Rifle Volunteers became the 1st Buckinghamshire Rifle Volunteer Corps (or the 3rd Volunteer Battalion, The Oxfordshire Light Infantry) and in 1908 they were re-designated the Buckinghamshire Battalion of the Oxfordshire & Buckinghamshire Light Infantry, in the new Territorial Force, with its Headquarters at Aylesbury but a detachment at Marlow. Several Buckinghamshire battalions were raised in World War I to serve on the Western Front. And when Europe was threatened once again with war in 1939, the Secretary of State for War, Leslie Hore-Belisha, doubled the Territorial Army overnight, the 2nd Bucks were raised in the southern half of the county excepting the High Wycombe Company which went to France with the 1st Bucks in 1940 and again as the 6th Beach Group on D-Day.

Owen Wethered's son Frank did not live at Remnantz – an uncle's widow who had out lived his father still occupied the house. He served with the Royal Warwickshire Regiment in the Great War and later commanded the 1st Bucks. Frank died in 1922, his ill health aggravated by having been gassed in World War I.

SUBSEQUENT HISTORY

My father inherited Remnantz in 1922. He was a Lieutenant in the Royal Navy and away on duty, so the house was let to a Mrs Harris, who ran it as a boarding house. In 1924 he married the daughter of a Brigadier General Baldwin, who had been killed at Gallipoli.

In May 1938 my parents attended the wedding in Marlow of a cousin, Ann Wethered, to James Ritchie, a banker and a TA Officer with the Buckinghamshire Battalion. Ann was the daughter of Colonel Joe Wethered, Chairman of the Brewery and a former Commanding Officer of the Gloucesters, who had served with distinction in World War I. This branch of the Wethered family was a military one, serving with the Gloucesters and the Royal Warwicks as well as the Oxfordshire & Buckinghamshire Light Infantry. While at the wedding, my parents decided to evict Mrs Harris, who had fallen into debt, before she did a runner, and go to live in Remnantz themselves instead. In December 1938 we moved in, the whole house having been redecorated in 1930s style.

During World War II, my father was away from 1940 for nearly four years in the Navy, and my mother had over 40 officers and refugees, staying, evacuated or billeted on her during that time. The house was nearly taken over at one point by the RAF - who were at nearby Medmenham - but our mother pulled up the drawbridge and said 'NO'! However, a compromise was reached whereby the Air Training Corps cadets could use part of the stable block as their headquarters. She also prevented the antique iron railings from the front of the house being wrenched from their fixings! Mother also held 'work parties' every Thursday afternoon when helpful friends came to make bandages from old sheets, and she was a staunch member of the WVS, now the WRVS.

During the war, my brothers who were seven and ten years older than I were already away at school. The elder was at Dartmouth Royal Naval College intent on following his father into the Royal Navy rather than keeping up with the military tradition of previous Wethereds. I remained at home. In the early 1900s an earlier Wethered had extended the east wing of Remnantz to house a new kitchen which replaced the original one in the cellar, and a servant's hall. Above this was a separate staircase where the men servants had had their rooms! This became the 'nursery wing' for me and a series of people who came to look after me, and I remember our food coming up in a little lift from the kitchen below. I can remember too, being carried down the back stairs to the cellar, built under the oldest part of the house, during air raids.

The war over, my father retired in 1949 and led a busy life in the town where so many of his predecessors had done the same. He died at Remnantz in 1981 and my mother in 1994. My elder brother Anthony, whose research and writings make up much of this article, died of Motor Neurone Disease there in 2005. His widow Diana sold the house in 2007 and now lives in a 1998 town house built on the site of what was once of the brewery.

To conclude this history of a house and its people, Remnantz now belongs to another Stephen, a well-known auctioneer of military artefacts, Stephen Bosley and his wife. During our time at Remnantz musket balls and uniform buttons were unearthed in what had been the parade ground of the College and which after World War II was turned back into a peaceful meadow with wild flowers and Guernsey Cows. The Bosleys are restoring the dear old house to its former glory and filling it with 'Things Military'; what could be a more fitting end to my story?

A recent picture of Remnantz, which is now the home of a well-known auctioneer.

Caroline Osborne

MAJOR
THE HON ARTHUR GEORGE CHILD VILLIERS
(1983-1969)
A Yeoman & Citizen of Distinction
Derek Marsh
(Trustee of Oxfordshire Yeomanry Trust & Manager for The Manor Charitable Trust, 1956-1996)

BIOGRAPHICAL NOTES

Arthur Villiers was born on 24th November, 1883, the second son of the 7th Earl of Jersey, who owned Middleton Park in Oxfordshire, where Arthur was born, and Osterley Park at Brentford. He was educated at Mortimer Preparatory School, Eton College and New College Oxford, where he joined the Bullingdon Club and obtained a 4th class degree in History. He later resided in London, first in Hackney and then in Leyton. In 1906, at the age of 23, he was introduced by Lord Mount Stephen to Gaspard Farrer, who was a partner in Barings Bank, and this led to Villiers entering Barings Office at Bishopsgate, where he started his career as a merchant banker and a successful investor of private funds. He subsequently became the Managing Director of Baring Brothers & Co, and was a founder member of The Manor Charitable Trustees (now the Villiers Park Educational Trust). He died on 28th May 1969.

GILLEMONT FARM & RIFLE WOOD

In April 2005 the Oxfordshire Yeomanry Trust, the Oxfordshire Yeomanry Association and members of No.5 (Queens's Own Oxfordshire Hussars) Signal Squadron (V) jointly held a memorial service at the newly erected memorial near Domart-sur-la-Luce, Amiens commemorating those who were killed in World War I at The Battle of Rifle Wood in April 1918, one of whom was Clarence Maasz. For that occasion Alan Saunders, who has since died, and was the son of Yeoman Corporal John Saunders MM, quoted some notes written by his mother's cousin Newell A'Bear, who had been with his father at Rifle Wood, and in which A'Bear said:

'There was a slight bank at the edge of the wood, and the man next to me (Maasz of 'A' Squadron) and I tried to make a trench behind it but the tree roots and blackberry bushes stopped us from making a good job. Maasz was killed when a bullet went through soft earth we had thrown up and hit him in the head. Shortly afterwards Major Villiers walked along the wood behind our chaps. He stopped by me and told me to bury Maasz, which I did when he had moved on. While he was talking to me a shell burst not far behind him. The blast made him bend forward, but I suppose his walking stick helped him to keep on his feet, he took no notice.'

The words 'he took no notice' hints that there was something special about the courage of this officer, showing a steeliness and indifference about the action around him. In fact, the record of Major Villiers as a soldier during World War I does indicate that my reading of those words could be correct.

The fighting at Gillemont Farm, near Lempire, in May 1917 led to the deaths of Major Valentine Fleming, Second Lieutenant Francis Silvertop and twenty-one men. In May of that year, Gillemont Farm was occupied by 'C' (Henley) Squadron of the Oxfordshire Yeomanry and, as it was regarded as a key position, it was imperative that it should remain in British hands. The Henley Squadron was commanded by Val Fleming with 'D' (Banbury) Squadron, commanded by Arthur Villiers, in support.

Major Fleming sent back a number of reports by runners, but Villiers felt that insufficient information was getting back to his support squadron, and as the farm was under severe bombardment he decided the only way to find out more was to go and find out for himself. He got through to the farm under heavy shell fire to find that Fleming and Silvertop were dead. Despite heavy casualties, having been inspired by Fleming, the morale of 'C' Squadron was unbroken and it was in full charge of the situation. Nevertheless, Villiers decided, on his own initiative, that he should remain at the farm to take command. The enemy was prevented from taking the farm and, for his action, Villiers was awarded a Distinguished Service Order.

The entry dated 20th May 1917 in the War Diary of the Queen's Own Oxfordshire Hussars records that, at 3.30 am:

'After Artillery preparation the enemy attacked the Farm and was repulsed with loss by our barrage and rifle fire. Two prisoners were captured. During the bombardment Major Valentine Fleming and 2nd Lt Silvertop were killed by a shell; three other ranks also killed by shell fire and five wounded, one of whom died during the day. Major Villiers took his Squadron part way up in support and himself went through the enemy barrage to find out the position and, finding the attack had been driven off, remained in command of C Squadron and sent his Squadron back'.

He was wounded twice and one of those occasions was

A group photograph showing members of the Bicester Troop, Queens Own Oxfordshire Hussars, on Salisbury Plain in 1914. Those present include Quarter Master Sergeant H.Swell and Lieutenant the Hon A.G.C.Villiers (seated, centre).

Oxfordshire Yeomanry Trust OXFYT310

on 1st April 1918 during the Battle of Rifle Wood when he was in command of the Oxford Hussars contingent of the Brigade. After the War, a member of the Queen's Own Oxfordshire Hussars, William A. Fenemore, wrote to him to thank him for a copy of the Regimental War History written by Adrian Keith-Falconer which Villiers had sent to him. Fenemore said '*I had often wondered whether you got through all right … and why I remembered you so well, Sir, was being with you on April 1st, 1918. You was wounded through the knee and you would not bother for us to dress it for you until we had got our objective*'.

Fenemore went on to describe the frightful fire that they went through to achieve what they had been ordered to do. The incident concerned took place during a brilliant and gallant counter-attack after a strong German offensive. It is recorded that Major Villiers rejoined the Regiment from England on 8th May 1918, no doubt after he had recovered from his wound, and also that on 26th July 1918 the bar to his DSO and was gazetted, for his bravery and leadership, on 1st April.

Later, in October 1918, the French awarded him the Croix de Guerre and he was mentioned in despatches on 17th December 1917 and again on 20th December 1918.

In Adrian Keith Falconers book *The Oxfordshire*

Hussars in The Great War of the offensive at Gillemont Farm on 1st April 1918 (following incidentally a long personal account of the operations by Arthur Villiers) the Divisional Commander (General Pitman) said '*The attack was carried through with dash and gallantry, and reflected the greatest credit on all ranks, especially when it is considered that the Division had been in action since 21st March, during which time they had suffered very heavy losses and not had time for rest or refitting.*'

And, the Commander of the Fifth Army (General Rawlinson) sent a telegram which said '*I am anxious to express to the 2nd Cavalry Division my admiration and warmest thanks for their successful counter-attack this morning, and I congratulate all ranks most heartily on their brilliant achievement. I fear they suffered heavily, but their victory has been invaluable at this critical juncture.*'

POST-WAR SERVICE TO THE REGIMENT

These honours and awards won during the Great War partly explain the sub-title 'A Yeoman of Distinction' at the start of this article. I say partly because, after bringing back the last of the Regiment from France and Flanders in May 1919, he went on to make an outstanding contribution to his old regiment and its men from 1919 to the time of his death on 29th May 1969, and even after that through a charitable trust that he and three other Old Etonians – Alfred Wagg, Gerald Wellesley and Edward Cadogan (later Sir Edward) – had founded in 1924. Through him, and with the help of soldiers who were with him in France and Flanders in The Great War, namely Sergeant Harry Stroud, Sergeant J. McFie, Corporal Nelson Bradshaw and Trooper Maurice French, annual re-unions were held from 1919 until 1965 in hotels in Banbury and, from 1966 to 1992, at the country headquarters of the Charitable Trust at Middleton Stoney.

Until his death there were two re-unions a year, one in November in Oxfordshire and one in summer in Leyton at the sports ground of the Eton Manor Boys' Club. At the latter wives were included, and a bowls match was played between the Yeomanry and the Old Boys of the Club. Besides these annual gatherings, a Yeomanry Welfare Fund was administered, help given when needed and he kept in touch personally with a great many old soldiers.

At his Memorial Service the eulogy was given by Sir George Schuster, who was persuaded by Villiers to join the Queen's Own Oxfordshire Hussars, and in the eulogy Schuster said 'He never forgot a personal connection. He never missed the chance to pay a personal visit or give help to anyone who needed his help and advice. I was always amazed at how he did it'.

THE ETON MANOR BOYS' CLUB

Arthur Villiers was a Citizen of Distinction for many reasons, but most prominently for his involvement with the above mentioned Trust and Boys' Club, the merchant bank Baring Brothers, his old school Eton College and his help to the boroughs of Hackney, Leyton and Leytonstone in East London.

The Eton Manor Boys' Club was founded on the site of Manor Farm in Hackney Wick by another Oxfordshire Yeoman, Gerald Wellesley in 1909. Shortly afterwards, he persuaded Villiers to become involved and, after Wellesley withdrew in the 1920s, Villiers became the leading light with both the Club, until it was closed in 1967, and with The Manor Charitable Trust that sponsored the Club. A fine club house was built in Hackney in 1913, opened by the Club's first president, Lord Roberts, and a magnificent 32 acre sports ground was developed in Leyton on a waste dumping site in the 1920s. The activities and sports in both these centres were numerous and moved with the times.

In the 1950s and 60s the Boys' Club's membership rose from 400 to 600 until it was restricted to 500 so that members could feel they were known by the staff. The Old Boys of the Club, who ran their own sporting and cultural activities, always numbered over 1,000. Two interesting points, as we near the 2012 Olympics, are that in the 1950s Villiers bought for the Club's running track the cinder track from Wembley Stadium used in the 1948 Olympics. Also the site of that Sports Ground will be part of the 2012 Olympics location. On that site, providing there will be no change of mind between now and the time of the Games, a war memorial to local youth and a tribute to Winston Churchill's wartime inspiration (which also links the Club with the Oxfordshire Yeomanry) will be able to be seen by some of those who attend the Games. This memorial, commissioned by Villiers, demonstrates his interest, love and, I think, his passion for his Regiment and the Club.

THE VILLIERS PARK EDUCATIONAL TRUST & OTHER CHARITABLE WORK

Emanating from the educational activities of the Boys' Club, which were encouraged by Villiers and another Old Etonian Manager of the Club Sir Edward Cadogan, was Villiers Park at Middleton Stoney, a residential education centre running courses for sixth formers from 1964 to 2001 when its work was transferred to its sister centre at Foxton near Cambridge and still continues today under the auspices of The Manor Charitable Trust – now named the Villiers Park Educational Trust. In the late 1960s Villiers was the motivator of this move from traditional boys' club activities to short term residential educational experiences for young people. They were developed and expanded after his death.

Through him a great many enterprises were brought to fruition in Hackney, Leyton and Leytonstone. The following are just a few examples. In Hackney much help was given to schools including Berkshire Road from which a bridge was built across a canal so that pupils could get onto the sports ground more quickly and financial help was given towards the building of the Hackney Free and Parochial School. In the 1920s he and Gerald Wellesley also fought a great legal battle with the Government, persuading it to build high rise flats elsewhere rather than take some of the green fields of Hackney Marshes which were used for football and other sports. In Leyton a floodlit red-gra playing field was provided, churches were helped to raise money by an offer of trebling amounts raised by the churches to a maximum of £3,000 and in Leytonstone, The Pastures Youth Club was built. For his imaginative ideas and tremendous generosity and he was made a Freeman of the Borough of Leyton in 1951 and of Hackney in 1955.

BARING BROTHERS & CO. LIMITED

Arthur Villiers returned to Barings after World War I and, having become Managing Director, he gained a most amazing reputation as an investor. He also strengthened the relationship between Barings, Rothschilds and Schroders, enabling very large transactions to be undertaken. Shortly after World War II, following a visit to Germany and seeing how they were starting to rebuild, he suggested buying a lot of their failing bonds. Barings did so at a low percent and they were sold at ten times their purchase price!

In the late 1960s Mr David Robarts, the chairman of

Arthur Villiers in later years, as shown in a portrait which was painted posthumously by Elsa Ayres in 1970 from a black and white photograph. A plaque attached to the frame states that the portrait was 'commissioned by comrades of the Queens Own Oxfordshire Hussars who served with him in France and Flanders from 1914 to 1918 as a lasting tribute for his kindness and friendship till the time of his death in May 1969'.
Derek Marsh

National Provincial Bank, which later amalgamated with the Westminster Bank to form 'NatWest', was being shown round the estate at Middleton Park, Middleton Stoney, Oxfordshire, which had once been owned by Lord Jersey, Villiers' father and which Arthur had bought back for The Manor Charitable Trust. While on the tour he commented 'I do not think Arthur has ever made a mistake investing'. He paused and thought on and then added, 'He must have done, as everyone does, but I cannot remember one'. Praise indeed from a friend and a banker in such a prominent position. Through his investing. he maintained the funds for the Boys' Club and the fund allocated for Oxfordshire Yeomanry matters. It was often said of him that he did not think five years ahead but fifty: outside of investing one example of this is that in the 1950s he had an electric car and an electric van!

WORK FOR ETON COLLEGE

Another example of his skill at investing was in connection with Eton College for which after leaving the school and particularly after returning from active service in World War I, he had a lot of time, encouraging links and sporting activities between Eton, Barings and the Eton Manor Clubs (Boys and Old Boys). Eton was left an endowment by Gaspard Farrer, a partner of Baring Bothers & Co Ltd, and Arthur Villiers became Chairman of the Farrer Trust. By shrewd and clever investment he multiplied the value of this fund enormously, so much so that the fund was able to pay for new developments including the building of two new boys' houses – subsequently named Farrer House and Villiers House – a new theatre, much needed work on the College Chapel and housing for school teaching staff.

After this ambitious building work was completed there was enough money left in the fund to keep up the maintenance of these properties. At Eton in the cloisters which have portraits of distinguished old boys his photograph is alongside that of The Right Honourable Alec Douglas-Home who was Prime Minister from October 1963 to October 1964.

ARTHUR VILLIERS IN WORLD WAR II

Arthur Villiers was highly involved on the home front during World War II between 1939 and 1945, and a few instances of his involvement are recorded here. When the war started, the Eton Manor Club in Hackney Wick was closed with some activities continuing on the Club's sports ground at Leyton. The Manor House behind the club, where Villiers lived, was turned into a Civil Defence Headquarters for the ARP, Army Cadets and the Home Guard. Arthur Villiers was a Major in the Home Guard under the Commanding Officer, Brigadier Sir Stuart Mallinson.

The club had a dental surgery in the Hackney building and that was converted into a small emergency hospital. The army moved onto the sports ground and many of its buildings were used by both the regulars and the Home Guard. The grounds became the starting point for large scale manoeuvres and the centre for regimental affairs. Villiers himself moved into the ground-keeper's house, where he stayed for the rest of his life. He had a dug-out constructed just outside and often slept in it.

There were close to 600 members of the Club in the armed forces and Arthur kept in touch with a very great many of these individuals writing personal notes to them all over the world. He set up, through friends, outposts for them to call into in India, Africa, Australia and Egypt. During the blitz he was often first on the scene and called in his war time management and ground staff to help. If he heard of a club member's house being bombed out he would have £10 handed to them and if a house had its windows and doors blasted in they received £5. These were very useful sums of money at that time.

One of his responsibilities for the Home Guard was

Arthur Villiers (left) and Gerald Wellesley during World War I.
Oxfordshire Yeomanry Trust OXFYT43

the recruiting of factory units and these formed two battalions, the 34th Walthamstow and the 35th Leyton. Later, both battalions along with six other battalions made up 'J' sector of the Home Guard, London District.

War time help to those in trouble was not confined to Hackney and Leyton as Barings had transferred to Stratton, Milcheldever, Hampshire, where during his visits he gave financial assistance to many of those who lived in the area.

There was very much more to this remarkable man, who touched the lives of so many, than what is recorded here. He was greatly respected and loved by those who were with him in the Great War as he did so much with and for them. Just listening to them and being aware of some of their letters to him and to each other is sufficient evidence of that, but their desire to appreciate collectively his kindnesses was also shown by gifts paid for by them and given to him on special occasions and anniversaries. These included a Georgian Silver Cup for him to use at the Eton Manor Boys' Club, a scaled model of the 32 acre Eton Manor Sports Ground, an onyx pen stand and a framed photograph of a group of Oxfordshire Yeomen following a tour of battlefields and cemeteries in France which he had organised for them. After his death they commissioned an oil painting (see photograph and caption) which now hangs at Villiers Park at Foxton, in Cambridgeshire.

At his funeral, a most poignant remark was one by a friend who at the end of it said to Sir George Schuster 'What I would like engraved on my tombstone is Thank God for Arthur Villiers.'

Arthur Collier in the uniform of the Queens Own Oxfordshire Hussars at Blenheim in 1911.
Oxfordshire Yeomanry Trust OXFYT284

SERGEANT-MAJOR ARTHUR COLLIER

Christopher Collier

The background to the Haldane Reforms will be well known to the majority of readers of this publication. Initiated after the Anglo Boer War by Richard Burdon Haldane, the Secretary of State for War, and administered to a large degree by Major General Douglas Haig, they were designed to establish a British Expeditionary Force and to attempt to provide the vast reserves of men necessary if Britain were to be involved in a continental war against nations like Germany with their huge manpower reserves brought about by universal conscription. A part-time volunteer organisation, known as the Territorial Force was also created on 1st April 1908, encompassing the reserve units of the Army, with the old militia units being transferred to the newly created Special Reserve.

As a small cog in this vast, new administrative machine, Staff Sergeant Major Arthur Collier was posted from the 18th Hussars to the 'Queen's Own Oxfordshire Imperial Yeomanry', on 1st September 1908. This made him one of the first senior members of the regular forces to join the new Territorial Force. He was, in fact, one of the first Permanent Staff Instructors to have served with the Territorial Force.

Arthur Collier was my great, great uncle, whom I discovered in my researches into my family tree. He is a man who I never met, but with whom I nevertheless strongly identify as a kinsman and as a former soldier. In the following article I hope to tell something about his military history and the history of Great Britain at the time; something about his involvement with the Oxfordshire Yeomanry and something of the social conditions which led a farmer's labourer from Wiltshire to have a 30 year career in the Army, serving three monarchs. I have followed the historical sources but if you detect an element of partiality in favour of someone who I believe represents all that is best in the professional British soldier, I beg you to forgive me.

EARLY YEARS

Arthur Collier was born in the small village of Dilton Marsh, near Westbury in Wiltshire, on 28th October 1872, the 35th year of Queen Victoria's reign. He was the fourth son Of Henry and Elizabeth Collier, and had seven brothers and three sisters. The Collier family had lived in and around Dilton since the latter part of the 17th century, and they were active in the cloth weaving trade. During his long life Arthur's father, Henry, was variously a cloth weaver, a gardener or a labourer, while Elizabeth was a weaver and homemaker for an eventual eleven children – a contribution not recognised on contemporary censuses – she was noted as just a 'wife'.

Conditions as the child of a cloth weaver in the latter part of the 19th century left little hope of a career as we might understand it today. Girls married or went into service and boys took the Queen's shilling or worked the land. Pensions and benefits did not exist. In 19th century censuses many names were recorded not under 'Household', but 'Institution' – the workhouse or 'parish house'. The working classes worked until they died. On one census page an 86 year old is listed as an 'Agricultural Labourer'.

This was the background to the path followed by Arthur. He, his elder brother Walter and his younger brother Job all enlisted during the Victorian era. Walter and Job went into the Highland Light Infantry. Job died in 1903 shortly after returning from the war in South Africa.

Walter (my Great Grandfather – who is a story in himself), also served in South Africa with the Imperial Yeomanry. His enlistment two weeks after the birth of his son Walter Lawrence (my grandfather) indicated, perhaps, his impatience with the early stages of babyhood; Walter died as a member of the Royal Defence Corps in 1917. The eldest brother of the family, Albert, served for 22 years in the Royal Navy from 1881 to 1903 and was recalled to the colours during World War I at the age of 50, serving in the Dardanelles. Two other brothers, Frank and Charley, also served during the Great War in the Devonshire Regiment and Royal Garrison Artillery respectively.

JOINING UP

On 21st November 1887, Arthur enlisted at Devizes Barracks before Sergeant William Moore of the 3rd (Militia) Battalion of the Wiltshire Regiment. Arthur stated his age as 18 years 1 month, but he was actually about 16. At 5 ft 7 inches tall and weighing 131 lbs, he was well built for a working class lad of his day, probably as a result of his country upbringing which was infinitely healthier than conditions in the towns and cities of Victorian England.

In 1887, the military was not the respectable career it is today. Despite the Cardwell reforms of the 1870s, which had introduced short service and attempted to embed the old numbered regiments into local communities by basing them on a county system, 'Tommy' was not universally respected and 'decent' girls would be warned against consorting with soldiers. Not for nothing would a future Field Marshal's mother cry, weeping, that 'she would rather bury him than see him in a red coat!' However,

Wiltshire Regiment cap badge.

A postcard view of the 'keep' at Devizes Barracks. This distinctive structure was, in effect, a red-brick version of the stone keep at Cowley Barracks.
Christopher Collier

needs must meant that boys like Arthur took the Queen's shilling. There was little else for them as the cottage cloth weaving industry of Wiltshire began to die out.

Arthur was sent off to Shorncliffe barracks to begin his service with the 14th Hussars, with an original Regimental number of 2748. On 16th October 1889 he transferred to the 18th Hussars after 1 year 329 days service. Upon his transfer to the 18th he was issued with a new Regimental Number, 3513 which would remain with him throughout his military career. This would not prevent some records having the inscription of some of his medals with his original regimental number.

SERVICE OVERSEAS

Arthur sailed to India on 19th November 1889 as a Private in the 18th Hussars - the rank of 'Trooper' for cavalry soldiers was introduced after World War I. He served at Ambala, near Chandigarh, not far in Indian terms from the North West Frontier, throughout 1890 and, on 7th April 1891 he received his first promotion to Lance Corporal – which as any ex - soldier will tell you is the hardest. Good Conduct pay followed in May 1891 and, some 2½ years later, he was raised to the rank of Corporal and was awarded a second increase in Good Conduct Pay.

For reasons that are not clear, he requested to revert

to the rank of Private on 12th May 1894. This is an annotation that is not unusual in Victorian Army records, but I have no details of why this steady and successful NCO should have asked for a return to the ranks. Certainly, on the day after his reversion to Private he was awarded another pay rise for Good Conduct and this would seem to rule out any disciplinary reason for his drop in rank. John Lucy in his classic book *There's a Devil in the Drum*, suggests that the Junior NCOs of the era were so harassed with work and duties that many felt happier as private soldiers! In January 1895 he was back as a Lance Corporal again, with further promotion to Corporal following in November 1897.

Meanwhile, his terms of service changed in April 1898, when he signed in his Service Record, 'I hereby elect to come under the new rules contained in Army Order Feb. 5th 1895'. It is assumed that with this he changed his initial Short Service of nine years with the Colours and three in Reserve to a longer term. At this time, the Regiment was stationed in Lucknow, 100 miles from Nepal. It is certain that Arthur experienced all the exotica and the tedium of Garrison life as part of the British Raj. It may then have come as a relief when on 15th October 1898 Arthur sailed with the Regiment after nearly nine years service in India, for South Africa, where the farmers of the Boer republics were in revolt against the Empire.

THE WAR IN SOUTH AFRICA

During the Boer War, Arthur was promoted first to Lance Sergeant in 1899 and then to Sergeant in 1900. This period was punctuated with much action. On 20th October 1899 the Regiment, commanded by Lieutenant Colonel Moller was involved in the Battle of Talana where the British cavalry were poorly handled and seem to have displayed alternate bouts of recklessness and inertia. Moller became isolated from the rest of the regiment and most of 'B' Squadron became prisoners of the Boers, including Arthur.

There is still some confusion about their fate. According to Abbott's volume on *DCM winners and the South African War Casualty Roll: Natal Field Force*, he and his comrades were held for six days before release. However, one South African expert to whom I have spoken thinks it unlikely that Boer forces would have released British prisoners at this stage of the war, and Colonel Malet, in his *Memoirs of the 18th Hussars*, states that the captured men were held in Pretoria until the fall of that town. Other accounts have it that he was captured while skirmishing before Ladysmith during the siege and held for seven months before making his escape. However,

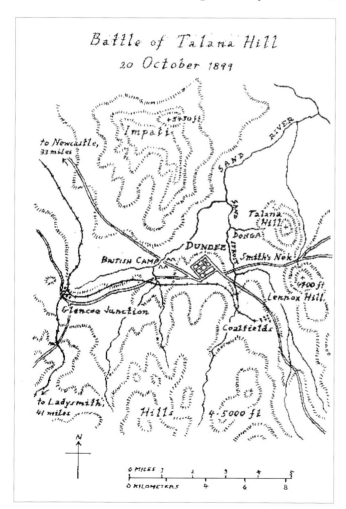

A sketch map of the 'Battle of Talana Hill', during the Boer War. *Christopher Collier*

as the records indicate that he did not qualify for the 'Defence of Ladysmith' clasp to his Queen's South Africa Medal, it would seem to show that he did not serve in Ladysmith. At any rate he was back with the regiment a year later.

Arthur makes some interesting contributions to *The 18th Hussars in South Africa* by Major Charles Burnett. I find these particularly fascinating in that the views of an 'other rank' were sought out by an officer for a book which was intended for publication. I would be interested to know the extent to which Arthur's words were edited or Bowdlerised, bearing in mind that his exposure to formal education must have been limited.

I would invite you to judge for yourselves in this account of the events of 2nd and 3rd November 1900 in which he was involved in the rescue of a wounded comrade. Major Burnett recalled that: *"Whilst covering a retirement, 'B' Squadron was fired upon and Privates Reid and Stewart hit. Stewart was in danger of capture – his horse having been shot – when Sgt. Collier, accompanied by Private Bracey galloped back and got him away".* Arthur's own account was as follows:

'On November 3rd we were retiring back to Middleburg, and my troop, under Lieut. Bayford, was doing rearguard to the squadron. During the retirement my half troop was holding a ridge when a mounted man came over the ridge we had just left, and we immediately fired a volley at him, but fortunately not hitting him and he still came on quite leisurely. Corporal Valpy, who was looking through his glasses, said he made him out to be one of our own men. Just then two more men came up on the same ridge; they dismounted and fired, and we all saw the man fall forwards on his horse's neck.

I jumped on my horse and taking Private Bracey with me we galloped out to assist him, but unfortunately his horse made off to the right, but we caught him up and found it was Private Stewart. I could tell he was badly hit somewhere, but we could get nothing from him as he appeared to be partly unconscious. So we lifted him onto the front of my saddle, and Bracey took his horse and rifle. The Boers meantime tried hard to get round us, but after a hard gallop we managed to get past them, and reached the regiment safely'.

The 18th Hussars were still in the area of Middleburg when a column was formed under Colonel Payne which today might be called an 'all arms' battle group. It consisted of half a squadron of the 18th Hussars, two guns and the Inniskilling Fusiliers. Arthur takes up the tale of this 'trek':

'On November 29th 1900 we went with a column under Colonel Payne. The mounted troops consisted of 50 men of 'B' Squadron under Captain Haag. On the 30th we marched to Goodhope. There was a good lot of sniping when we started, and it appeared that one of the kopjes in

the direction we had to go was strongly held. All the guns were brought to bear on it and then Captain Haag with about 30 men made a dash for it; we had one man wounded going across the open veldt. We dismounted and climbed to the top of the kop with the usual result; you could just see what few Boers there were disappearing in the distance. We arrived in camp at 1 pm without further incident. At 2 pm a party of 30 men of the infantry with about 15 wagons was sent to a farm about 3 miles away, beyond the outposts, to bring in mealies etc. I went with this party with 6 men and after scouting through the farm and the ground beyond it, I retired to a small wood where we could keep a good lookout, without being seen ourselves.

We had been there about 1 ½ hours when two parties of Boers about 30 strong came out of a donga, two miles to our front and galloped towards us. Mounting one of my men to go and warn the officer in charge, I took up a position at the edge of the wood with the others. When they arrive about 1,500 yards from me they halted and sent 3 or 4 men on in advance, whilst they came on slowly in rear. We waited until their scouts arrived within 500 yards, when we put a volley into them and then fired 'independent' as fast as we could at both parties, with the result that they all galloped away to their right, leaving two of their horses behind them. Whether the men were wounded or not I could not tell. I sent Private Bowman to my left flank to watch them, and in the meantime the officer came up at a double with a few men, and I told him the strength of the enemy, and he said he should retire at once, and I was to try and keep them back until he reached the outpost.

Private Bowman came in to tell me that the Boers were working round my left flank, so leaving one man to watch my right; I took the others to the left. As soon as we appeared in the open we were met with a very sharp fire, but quickly dismounted and sending the horses out of range, as there was no cover, we kept up a steady fire whilst the wagons were reaching camp. As soon as we commenced to run to our horses the Boers came galloping after us, so we quickly dropped down again, and after firing a few rounds at them, they took cover and we retired again with the same result, but this time they had reached the wood we had previously occupied, and I signalled at once for the horses to come to us and we made a run for it.

One of the horses was shot before we could get mounted, but putting the man up in front of another, we just waited a bit to give him a start, and then made a rush for it, and I don't think anyone was sorry when the outpost was reached. All the men worked very well, especially Private Dorey, who was holding the horses (it was his first time under fire), and Private Bracey. On December 1st we retired to Middleburg, having one man, Corporal Cluer, slightly wounded on rearguard on the way.'

On 14th April 1901, The London Gazette contained the following entry: 'The King has further been pleased to approve of the grant of the Medal for Distinguished Conduct in the Field to the undermentioned Soldiers in recognition of their gallant conduct during the operations in South Africa - 18th Hussars. 3513 Lance-Sergeant Collier'.

It is hard to know for which particular act Arthur was honoured, possibly the rescue of Private Stewart or maybe for his general gallant conduct. It was later reported, in his obituary, that Arthur was recommended for the Victoria Cross for his rescue of Private Stewart, but refused the award as his colleague was not to be so honoured. It is an intriguing story but it is unlikely that after more than 100 years, the truth will be known. That Arthur was a gallant and resourceful NCO is in no doubt.

Arthur reengaged to complete 21 years service and was promoted to SSMRR on December 21st 1901. In 1902 the Hussars returned to England and 'Home' service began in November of that year at Aldershot – 'Home of the British Army'.

The 18th Hussars, now named 'Princess of Wales' Own Regiment' moved to York in 1904 and on November 6th Arthur married Ada Gilbank at St. Helen Stonegate York. Little is known of their time together except that they were still together in 1911, living at 35 Market Place Henley. His occupation is listed as 'Soldier. Permanent Staff of the QOO Hrs'. I am still attempting to research this period of Arthur's life. They had no children. Arthur was now 32 years old and had spent 17 of those years as a soldier. Three years later his Long Service and Good Conduct Medal was awarded, along with a gratuity. Arthur had completed his '20 years of undetected crime'.

TO THE OXFORDSHIRE YEOMANRY
In August 1905, Arthur's final promotion as a 'Regular' was to Staff Sergeant Major and on 1st September 1908, on completion of his 21 years of service; he was posted to the Oxfordshire Imperial Yeomanry as a SSM Sergeant Instructor with 'C' Squadron at Henley-on-Thames. He was one of the first 'Regulars' to be posted to a Yeomanry Regiment since the Territorial force had been created. The Squadron was commanded by a man who was to make his mark on British and world history – Winston Spencer Churchill – and had detachments at Watlington, Thame and Goring-on-Thames.

Life with the Yeomanry must have seemed very different from the strict discipline of the Regular Army, but it seems that Arthur quickly won the respect and affection of both officers and men as the Squadron carried out its drill nights, weekends and summer camps. Papers from the Winston Churchill archive held by Churchill College, Cambridge, show SSM Collier as the organizer of the day-to-day business of the Squadron. He was based in the White House, Henley-on-Thames, and correspondence shows that in April 1909 he went to London to visit Major Churchill at his office at the Board of Trade. He organized range days for the Squadron's musketry practice and Inter-Squadron Shooting matches, and the training of recruits. He also handled the day-to-day finances, receiving cash for marksmanship pay and paying the rent on the Squadron premises.

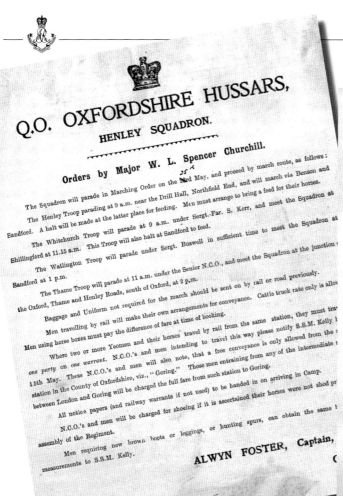

Q.O. OXFORDSHIRE HUSSARS,

HENLEY SQUADRON.

Orders by Major W. L. Spencer Churchill.

The Squadron will parade in Marching Order on the 23rd May, and proceed by march route, as follows:

The Henley Troop parading at 9 a.m. near the Drill Hall, Northfield End, and will march via Benson and Sandford. A halt will be made at the latter place for feeding. Men must arrange to bring a feed for their horses.

The Whitchurch Troop will parade at 9 a.m. under Sergt.-Far. S. Kerr, and meet the Squadron at Shillingford at 11.15 a.m. This Troop will also halt at Sandford to feed.

The Watlington Troop will parade under Sergt. Buswell in sufficient time to meet the Squadron at Sandford at 1 p.m.

The Thame Troop will parade at 11 a.m. under the Senior N.C.O., and meet the Squadron at the junction the Oxford, Thame and Henley Roads, south of Oxford, at 2 p.m.

Baggage and Uniform not required for the march should be sent on by rail or road previously.

Men travelling by rail will make their own arrangements for conveyance. Cattle truck rate only is allow

Men using horse boxes must pay the difference of fare at time of booking.

Where two or more Yeomen and their horses travel by rail from the same station, they must tra one party on one warrant. N.C.O.'s and men intending to travel this way please notify S.S.M. Kelly 15th May. These N.C.O.'s and men will also note, that a free conveyance is only allowed from the station in the County of Oxfordshire, viz., "Goring." Those men entraining from any of the intermediate between London and Goring will be charged the full fare from such station to Goring.

All notice papers (and railway warrants if not used) to be handed in on arriving in Camp.

N.C.O.'s and men will be charged for shoeing if it is ascertained their horses were not shod pr assembly of the Regiment.

Men requiring new brown boots or leggings, or hunting spurs, can obtain the same measurements to S.S.M. Kelly.

ALWYN FOSTER, Captain,

Henley-on-Thames,
April, 1908.

Q. O. O. HUSSARS,

(Imperial Yeomanry).

HENLEY SQUADRON.

Orders for day of assembly at Permanent Duty, 1905.

The Members of the Henley Squadron will join a special train (see particular below) in marching order on June 5th, 1905. The fare, for man and horse, from the stations specified, will be defrayed by Government, the excess fare from stations outside the County of Oxon will be chargeable to those travelling from such stations. Each man must be at the station selected by him at least half-an-hour before the time the train is due to start, and must produce his railway warrant and notice paper. A baggage wagon will be attached to the train, but men are advised to take as little baggage as possible to camp. Men coming from stations other than those mentioned, must, if two or more reside near that station, travel together. Cattle trucks only are allowed, so men must be prepared to pay the difference of fare between cattle trucks and horses boxes if using the latter.

N.C.O's and men travelling by road will arrange to arrive in Camp not later than 2 p.m.

*Depart Slough	....	9.15
* ,, Maidenhead	....	9.35
,, Henley	....	10.5
,, Pangbourne	......	.11.5
,, Didcot	....	11.35
Arrive Woodstock	....	12.30

* Stations from which excess fares are chargeable.

By Order

Alwyn Foster, Captain,

Henley Squadron.

Detailed Squadron Orders issued to members of the Henley Squadron, Queens Own Oxfordshire Hussars, in connection with the transport of men and horses to Yeomanry training camps. Note that the Yeoman were expected to travel in cattle trucks, those wishing to travel in the relative luxury of a horse box being expected to pay the difference in fare!

Oxfordshire Yeomanry Trust

Each year, the Permanent Staff of the Regiment competed amongst themselves for the 'Dugdale Cup'; a prestigious and handsome trophy initiated by Major Arthur Dugdale and awarded for excellence in musketry. This was won by Arthur during the course of the competition on 13th & 14th September 1909 at Bicester. It is heartening to think that Arthur's expertise rubbed off on the rest of 'C' Squadron. A newspaper report from 1911 tells of the squadron 'sweeping the boards' at the annual regimental rifle meeting:

'The annual Rifle meeting of the QOOH was held at Bicester on August 9th & 10th, when the Henley Squadron did exceedingly well and even surpassed their brilliant performances of last year. ...Lieut. Fleming and the other officers as well as Sergt. Major Collier, who have taken such a keen interest in the men's shooting, have every reason to be proud of the squadron's achievements and are to be congratulated on such conspicuous success'.

The Dugdale Challenge Cup awarded for excellence in musketry. *Oxfordshire Yeomanry Trust OXFYT593*

Arthur Collier on horseback.   *Christopher Collier*

THE GREAT WAR

War came again and the Yeomanry mobilised. On September 20th 1914, Arthur sailed to France aboard *SS Bellerophon* from Southampton with the British Expeditionary Force as SSM of 'C' Squadron Queen's Own Oxfordshire Hussars, commanded by Major C. R. I. Nicholl. Two days later they arrived at Dunkirk and disembarked. The Regiment moved east to Hazebrouck on 29th September and to Strazeele on 3rd October 1914. The Yeomanry then formed an advance guard, moving north towards the Mont des Cats in Flanders. It was here that 'C' Squadron became the first Territorials to come under fire in the Great War.

On 30th October 1914 the Regiment was ordered to Neuve Eglise, (Nieuwkerke), as part of the 1st Cavalry Division. During the final throes of 'The Race to the Sea' the Oxfordshire Hussars fought in what is now known as the 1st Battle of Ypres. Each of the Regiment's Squadrons took its turn to defend Messines against the German advance. 'C' Squadron manned barricades in the centre of the little town under shell and machine gun fire during the night of 31st October – 1st November, being relieved at 5 am by the 18th Hussars – Arthur's old regiment. The next evening, they withdrew down the road to Wulverghem but were soon turned out again to counter attack to cover the retirement of British troops from Messines. This contribution of the Yeomanry to the 1st Battle of Ypres is often forgotten nowadays, with most attention going to the admittedly stirring achievements of the London Scottish.

Static warfare was now becoming the rule and trenches were occupied between Wulverghem and Wytschaete on 2nd November 1914. These were mere slit trenches and bore no resemblance to the sophisticated defences and dugouts of later in the war. The regiment spent the next two days under quite heavy fire in this position. Christmas 1914 was uneventful, and January 1915 saw promotion for Arthur to the new rank of Warrant Officer Class 2. Two weeks later the Regiment moved to Ypres again and manned trenches near Zillebeke during the bitterly cold winter of 1914-15.

With the coming of spring the Germans attacked again at Ypres in April 1915, using poison gas for the first time in the war. During this 2nd Battle of Ypres the Yeomanry was ordered up to Ypres from the reserves. They moved into the line at Boesinge on 25th April, moving to between Potijze and Wieltje on 28th April 1915.

The spring and summer of 1915 found the QOOH in trenches at Vlamertinghe and Zouave Wood near Hooge – a renowned hot spot. Hopes of a breakthrough at Loos in September – one of many for which the cavalry had trained – were soon dashed. New Year 1916 was spent in trenches at Vermelles. It was becoming plain that this was no war for cavalry.

In the event, 1916 was destined to be Arthur's last year at war. On 14th January his name appeared in the *London Gazette* in a long list of DCM winners and on 11th March the Gazette published the citation for his second award of the DCM:

'3513 Squadron Serjeant-Major A. Collier, 18th Hussars (attached Permanent Staff, Oxfordshire Hussars, T.F.) For conspicuous gallantry and devotion; he brought in six wounded men from in front of the trenches under a heavy fire, the men having been left out from the previous day's engagement. He has invariably shown great bravery and coolness under fire, and set a fine example to all ranks'.

It would be interesting to attempt to pin down when this particular incident occurred. Given the delay in gazetting awards, it could have been during 1915 or even late 1914. The award was later converted to that of a Military Cross and Arthur was promoted to Regimental Sergeant Major on 3rd April 1916.

The QOOH spent summer on and around the Somme, preparing for the elusive breakthrough, but by November of that year it was obvious that RSM Collier's health had broken. He had spent 2 years and 66 days on active service in France and Belgium with, it seems, little or no leave. On November 22nd he was moved down the line to 4th Cavalry Field Ambulance. He complained of a sore throat and loss of voice. At this point he hoped to be able to return to his Regiment soon but was sent to Etaples to 24 General Hospital and then to England aboard the hospital ship *Cambria*.

In his comprehensive history *The Oxfordshire Hussars in the Great War* (1927) Adrian Keith-Falconer wrote:

'During the first eighteen months of the war he had been a pillar of strength to 'C' Squadron, and a constant help and support, first to Major Nicholl and then to Major Val Fleming his squadron leaders who always thought very highly of him. His promotion to RSM in February 1916... was a serious loss to his old squadron but he never forgot his old friends there and always took a special interest in their welfare and efficiency. The perpetual office work at Headquarters was not much to his taste; his greatest wish was for real cavalry fighting and a chance to use his sword, failing which he was happiest in the front trenches. If perhaps he seemed rather stern and grim to those who did not know him well, especially to young officers and men, he was always popular with the Serjeants and respected by the senior officers. He was a fine soldier and a brave man'.

He spent time at the Military Hospital in Lewisham, London and at Eggington Hall Derbyshire, a convalescent home owned by Viscount Valentia, but his condition deteriorated and he was discharged from the Army on 9th January 1917 at York after 29 years and 50 days service. The officer who signed his papers noted that he was:

'A man of highest character and a very gallant soldier'.

Arthur intended to live at 288 Kings Road, Kingston upon Thames, the home of his brother in law, Joseph Pocock. He was discharged with a pension of 40/- (£2) per week plus 3/6 (17.5p) for his DCM. On 17th April 1917, Arthur's Military Cross was gazetted and, not long after, he moved to his brother-in-law's house in Kingston.

Arthur Collier died on 1st June 1917 at 12 Gordon Road Kingston, of tuberculosis and exhaustion brought on by war service, aged 45 years. His last hours were witnessed by Joseph Pocock, who had married Arthur's sister Leonora in 1902. His death came just two days after he had heard of the death in action of Major Valentine Fleming DSO, MP, his former Squadron Commander in the Queen's Own Oxfordshire Hussars. Phillip Fleming wrote that: "He had a tremendous regard for Val, as Val had for him – for he was a really fine type of cavalry soldier".

Arthur is buried in Henley-on-Thames Cemetery. His funeral, with full military honours and attended by many officers, NCOs and local dignitaries, was reported in The Henley Standard on 8th June 1917:

'By his death the country has lost one of those fine non-commissioned officers, who are the backbone of the British Army. He was a soldier who knew his business thoroughly, of dauntless courage and of constant thought for his comrades ... He came to Henley some 7 or 8 years ago as Squadron Serjeant Major to the Oxfordshire Yeomanry and very quickly won the love and admiration of officers and men alike and these feelings were very considerably increased when the Regiment went on active service and all ranks saw what a great soldier their SSM was'.

Family members present included his brothers; Albert, a Petty Officer in the Royal Navy, Charley, a Bombardier in the Royal Garrison Artillery and Frank, a Private in the Devonshire Regiment. Arthur is commemorated on the War Memorials at Dilton Marsh and Henley-on-Thames. His spurs are interred with him. Cavalry to the last. His memorial reads:

In loving memory of our dear brother
R.S.M. A. Collier M.C. D.C.M.
18th Hussars and Oxfordshire Yeomanry.
Died June 1st 1917, aged 45 years.
Respected by all, loved by many.
A faithful friend to all, noble and
courageous though unassuming.
A modest hero and an ideal soldier.
For his country his life he gave
His end was perfect peace.

Arthur's gravestone can still be seen in Henley-on-Thames churchyard.
Christopher Collier

Sergeant Major Colliers medals, reflecting his distinguished service during the Boer War and in World War I.

Private Collection

PHOTO FEATURE: SOME BADGES & BUTTONS

The Royal Artillery: Like the RAOC, the Royal Artillery has many links with Oxfordshire, No.252 Heavy Battery having been recruited locally during World War II while, in that same conflict, the Oxfordshire Yeomanry became an anti-tank regiment. The RA badge is simple, but effective, being a field gun with two Latin mottoes, *Ubique* ('Everywhere') and *Quo fas et Gloria Ducant* ('Where Fame and Glory Lead').

The Royal Irish Rifles: In common with several other Irish regiments, the Royal Irish Rifles badge depicted an Irish harp below a crown, with the motto *Quis Separabit* ('who can separate us'). The regiment was re-styled 'The Royal Ulster Rifles' in 1920, and it has latterly been merged with the Royal Irish Regiment.

The Army Ordnance Corps: The Royal Army Ordnance Corps was formed in 1918, prior to which the Officers had been assigned to the Army Ordnance Department, while the warrant officers, NCOs and soldiers had belonged to the Army Ordnance Corps. The AOC badge was based on the arms of the Board of Ordnance, with its three non-fitting cannon balls. The RAOC is now an integral part of the Royal Logistical Corps.

The Irish Volunteers: An 'Irish Volunteer' button as worn by some of the Easter rebels during the 1916 Dublin rising. This 'crownless' harp motif was subsequently adopted by the Free State Army as a standard uniform button.

The 5th Royal Irish Lancers: The 'Harp & Crown' was adopted by many Irish regiments, including the 5th Royal Irish Lancers. This small, right-facing angel harp was a collar badge.

The Royal Army Ordnance Corps - The post-World War II version of the Royal Army Ordnance Corps cap badge with King's crown and lugged fixing. The Latin motto *Sua tela tonanti* is usually translated as 'Thundering forth his weapons'.

The Royal Dublin Fusiliers: A pair of Royal Dublin Fusiliers collar badges. The elephant and tiger reflect the regiment's long association with India.

Transport Section. 43rd Lt. Infantry. Dublin. 25th July 1922.

The 'Transport Section' of the 1st Battalion Oxfordshire & Buckinghamshire Light Infantry in Dublin on 25th July 1922.
Oxfordshire & Buckinghamshire Light Infantry Museum archives

THE OXFORDSHIRE & BUCKINGHAMSHIRE LIGHT INFANTRY IN IRELAND 1919-23

Stanley C. Jenkins MA

It used to be said that the British army had two 'spiritual homes', one of these being India while the other was Ireland. The protection of India was, for many years, the army's principal overseas task, the long association with the Raj being marked, to this day, by the large number of Urdu, Hindi or Arabic names that have entered into the English language. As far as Ireland is concerned, the relationship with the army was longer, more complex and perhaps more controversial. In historical terms, Ireland was a major recruiting ground for the British army – so much so that, at various times, the regular army was composed largely of Irishmen. In the early 19th century, for example, the 43rd and the 52nd Light Infantry seems to have been at least fifty per cent Irish, and many of the regiment's most famous figures were Irishmen, or of Irish descent. One thinks, for example, of Colonel William Rowan, of Metropolitan Police fame, who was a native of County Antrim, while Bugler Hawthorne, who won the VC at Delhi during the Indian Mutiny, was born at Maghera in County Londonderry.

HISTORICAL BACKGROUND

Ireland had been linked to the English crown since 1171, when Henry II, armed with a Papal Bull from Pope Adrian IV, entered Dublin to receive homage from his vassal Richard de Clare, who had married the King of Leinster's daughter and thereby inherited the throne of Leinster. Thereafter, Ireland was seen as an integral part of the Kingdom of England, although wars or rebellions erupted at various times, notably during the reign of Elizabeth I, when Hugh O'Neil, the Earl of Tyrone – 'a lonely, grand, tragic figure' – attempted to weld the fractious Gaelic tribes into a modern army which could face the English on equal terms; in the 1590s, his men were said to be wearing red coats and morion helmets, 'like English soldiers'[1].

In the following century a widespread rebellion in Ireland precipitated the English Civil War which, in turn, led to Oliver Cromwell's punitive Irish campaign of 1649-50, Religious differences had, by that time, poisoned relations between England and Ireland – the English having become enthusiastic Protestants whereas most of the Irish had remained Roman Catholics. Henceforth, religious strife would be an inevitable concomitant of Ireland's political troubles.

In 1689 the deposed King James II brought further troubles to Ireland when he invaded the island with French assistance and proceeded to make Catholicism

A member of the Oxfordshire & Buckinghamshire Light Infantry on guard duty in Ireland during the period of 'The Troubles'.

Oxfordshire & Buckinghamshire Light Infantry Museum archives

the official religion. Over two thousand Irish Protestants were condemned to death as 'traitors' and this made civil war inevitable. At length, the English intervened in support of their co-religionists – the Jacobites and their French allies being utterly defeated at the Battle of the Boyne in July 1690. A further rebellion in 1798, although inspired by the egalitarian ideals of the French Revolution, ended in sectarian strife and, after appalling outrages had been committed by both sides, the Irish Yeomanry and a small force of regulars subdued the rebels at the Battle of Vinegar Hill.

These complex and tragic events placed the Protestants firmly in charge of Irish affairs, the Irish Parliament in Dublin being a corrupt and self-serving institution which was not, by any stretch of the imagination, representative of the Irish people. Realising that the 1798 Rebellion had been driven by a genuine and deeply-felt sense of injustice, successive British governments attempted to alleviate Ireland's grievances, an important step being taken on 1st January 1801 when, 'after bribery on a scale such as history has seldom witnessed', an Act of Union came into force between England and Ireland. It was anticipated that Catholic emancipation would immediately be granted by the Westminster Parliament, though in the event this entirely reasonable measure did not come into force until 1829.

It is generally considered that, by the 19th century, about 70-75 per cent of the Irish population were Roman Catholics, while the remaining 25-30 per cent were Protestants – the Protestants being themselves divided, insofar as the Nonconformists, who were particularly strong in north-eastern Ireland, refused to accept the authority of the established Church of Ireland. Generally speaking, the Irish Protestants, both Anglicans and Nonconformists, thought of themselves as British citizens who lived in an integral part of the United Kingdom, whereas the Catholics favoured what came to be known as 'Home Rule' – in other words the repeal of the Union and the establishment of a devolved Irish government in Dublin.

By the end of the 19th century the Irish Nationalists, led by Charles Stuart Parnell (1846-91), a Protestant landowner, had become a major force in British politics, the Parnellites being able to hold the balance of power to such an extent that 'The Irish Question' dominated the workings of Parliament. Ireland had moreover, become a major party-political issue insofar as the Liberals favoured Home Rule whereas the Tories were unswerving supporters of the Union and the Church of Ireland. Having made unsuccessful attempts to introduce Home Rule Bills in 1886 and 1892, it appeared that, in 1912, the Liberals would finally be able to impose this deeply-divisive measure. At that juncture, however, the Irish

Haulbowline Island, in Cork Harbour, was adapted for use as a naval dockyard during the Napoleonic War, and its facilities were progressively improved during the Victorian period. When the dockyard was being built, a further 30 acres of ground was reclaimed, bringing the total area of the island to around 60 acres. A Martello tower was provided for defensive purposes while, in 1894, a narrow gauge railway was constructed to link the various wharves, basins and store houses. Note the square-rigged warships in this circa 1860s view. *Oxfordshire & Buckinghamshire Light Infantry Museum archives*

College Green, in Dublin, showing the equestrian statue of King William III, the victor of the Boyne, which was blow up by the IRA in 1946.   *Oxfordshire & Buckinghamshire Light Infantry Museum archives*

The entrance to Dublin Castle, showing the Guard Room.   *Oxfordshire & Buckinghamshire Light Infantry Museum archives*

Ship Street Barracks in Dublin, during the late Victorian period.

Protestants in north-eastern Ireland declared that Home Rule would be 'disastrous to the material well-being' of Ireland, subversive 'to civil and religious freedom … and perilous to the unity of the Empire'[2]. Vowing to defend their 'cherished position of equal citizenship within the United Kingdom' they raised an 'Ulster Volunteer Force' of 100,000 men and swore to use 'all means which may be found necessary' to oppose the Home Rule Bill.

Faced with this thinly-veiled threat of violence, Herbert Asquith, the Liberal Prime Minister, prevaricated – his discomfiture being magnified by the so-called 'Curragh Mutiny', when the commander of the Third Cavalry Brigade and fifty-seven of his officers announced that they would resign their commissions rather than take offensive action against Ulster[3]. Meanwhile, a pro-Home Rule and largely Roman Catholic force known The Irish Volunteers had been formed to oppose the Ulster Volunteers. It appeared that civil war was about to commence between the rival factions in Ireland, but in the event the outbreak of World War I in August 1914 ensured that the 'Irish Question' was, albeit temporarily, subsumed by an immeasurably greater conflict.

THE BLACK & TANS

Although the Great War came to an end on 11th November 1918, there was little peace in Ireland. The prolonged agitation for Irish 'Home Rule' had, for many years, been conducted in perfect legality by the Irish Nationalist Party which, in 1914, had committed itself to the common struggle against Germany. Undeterred by this pledge, a small group of extreme Irish nationalists had staged a sacrificial rising in Dublin in Easter 1916. This open rebellion, in time of war, was inevitably followed by a series of executions that enraged the Roman Catholic population of Ireland, and resulted in increasing support for the idea of complete separation from England[4].

The Easter Rising and its aftermath changed the nature of the Home Rule movement, which henceforth sought a final and irrevocable break with England. The survivors of the Easter Rising were imprisoned for the duration of the war with Germany, but on their release the '*Sinn Feiners*' created a new, undercover organisation known as 'The Irish Republican Army' in order the continue what they now regarded as an outright war with England. In consequence, the Easter Rising was followed by a more widespread rebellion in 1919.

'War', as practised by the IRA, consisted chiefly of ambushes, shoot-outs and random murders – members of the Royal Irish Constabulary being among their first victims. On 21st January 1919, for example, Constable Patrick O'Connell and Constable James O'Donnell were shot dead by IRA gunmen while escorting a cart load of gelignite to a quarry at Soloheadbeg in County

A detailed view showing members of 'F' Company, 43rd Light Infantry, in front of the small, cottage-type structure which can also be seen in the view of Ship Street Barracks opposite. The date is circa 1894.

Oxfordshire & Buckinghamshire Light Infantry Museum archives

Members of the regiment pose for the camera at Beggars Bush Barracks, Dublin, in 1897. Beggars Bush came under attack during the Irish Civil War, when members of the IRA attempted to seize the barracks from the newly-created Free State army.

Oxfordshire & Buckinghamshire Light Infantry Museum archives

Tipperary, their weapons and explosives being taken by the rebels. A few weeks later, on 30th March, retired District Inspector John Milling was murdered in his own home and, thereafter, Irish policemen were targeted in increasing numbers.

Under these circumstances Sir Hamar Greenwood, the uncompromising Irish Secretary, and Prime Minister David Lloyd George, sought to implement a more robust form of policing. Incensed by the activities of the Irish Republican Army, the government reinforced the Royal Irish Constabulary by recruiting former soldiers from the British army, who were known colloquially as 'The Black & Tans' because their uniforms were originally a mixture of army khaki and RIC dark green. In a letter to *The Times*, dated 16th November 1920, an Irish correspondent explained that, 'when they first came over there was not sufficient uniform of the dark green pattern to equip them, and they were partially fitted-out in khaki, perhaps a tunic or trousers of that material, with the RIC cap – hence the designation Black & Tan'. The letter-writer added that, the shortage having ceased, the men were soon attired in rifle green RIC uniforms and there was 'nothing to distinguish them from the RIC of yesterday', although in conduct there 'was a vast difference' – some of the new recruits

being ill-disciplined and poorly-motivated, while their military training hardly fitted them for police work in the sensitive conditions which pertained throughout much of Ireland.

Meanwhile, an additional force known as the 'Auxiliary Division of the Royal Irish Constabulary', which was composed of former British officers with first-class military records, had been recruited, ostensibly as 'officer cadets' who would be attached to the Royal Irish Constabulary.

In view of their commissioned status the Auxiliaries were better paid than the rank and file RIC personnel, and it was originally intended that they would provide a disciplined and highly-motivated 'officer class', though in reality they soon became a law unto themselves. Armed to the teeth with Webley 0.45 inch revolvers and Lee-Enfield 303 rifles, swathed in bandoliers and wearing military tunics and distinctive black or khaki Tam O'Shanter bonnets, they roared around the countryside in Crossley tenders, firing recklessly and intimidating any civilians who had the misfortune to get in their way. In effect the RIC Auxiliary Division was employed as a striking force to hunt down the IRA and its 'flying columns'[5], this 'Irish gendarmerie' being the government's principal weapon in the campaign against

Another glimpse of barracks life in southern Ireland in the halcyon days before the 'Troubles'. It is believed that this large stone building was part of Beggars Bush Barracks.   *Oxfordshire & Buckinghamshire Light Infantry Museum archives*

An unidentified paddle steamer moored near St Patrick's Bridge, Cork, during the Victorian period. Despite (or perhaps because of) the presence of a large Protestant community, Cork and the surrounding area became a centre of rebel activity during the 'Troubles'. There were also some ugly sectarian attacks, one of the worst incidents being the murder of a Church of Ireland clergyman on the doorstep of his father's rectory at Murragh.

Oxfordshire & Buckinghamshire Light Infantry Museum archives

the rebels – although it was envisaged that the army would be held in reserve, and in these circumstances there was a pressing requirement for additional troops in Ireland.

THE REGIMENT MOVES TO CORK & LIMERICK

The Oxfordshire & Buckinghamshire Light Infantry was in Ireland in considerable strength by 1919, the 3rd (Special Reserve) Battalion having left England *en route* for Victoria Barracks, Cork, on 1st March 1919. At that time the 3rd Battalion comprised about 300 men, but as new recruits continued to arrive the size of the Battalion increased to 1,000 men. The 2nd Battalion travelled from Oxford to Cork on 30th July and, on arrival, it absorbed the 3rd Battalion, which was deemed to have been disembodied on 1st August 1919[6].

Members of the 1st Battalion joined the 52nd in Victoria Barracks in the following November, but in December, the 43rd were told that they would shortly be moving to Ballyvonare Camp near Buttevant. The move was accomplished on 8th January 1920, although in the following June the 43rd were transferred from Ballyvonare to Limerick, where they occupied a number of different barracks, including Castle Barracks, Strand Barracks and 'New Barracks Camp'[7]. Thus, by the beginning of 1920, the Oxfordshire & Buckinghamshire

Light Infantry was present in considerable strength in the disaffected south-western Province of Munster, the 1st Battalion being stationed in Limerick, while the 2nd Battalion was concentrated in Cork.

The men of the 2nd battalion found that their first few months spent in Ireland were surprisingly quiet, although on 5th September 1919 around sixty members of the regiment were called out to assist at the scene of a major fire at Douglas Mills near Cork. It is gratifying to note that the owners of the premises sent £20 to the commanding officer for distribution among the soldiers in recognition of the help that they had provided – the money being sufficient to pay each man the not inconsiderable sum of 6s. 8d. each[8].

The 2nd Battalion carried out its first aggressive patrol in support of the RIC on 28th September 1919, following the shooting of two police constables at Berrings. The regimental *Chronicle* reported that three officers and 20 other ranks paraded at 16.45 hrs and proceeded in four lorries to King Street and Union Quay RIC Barracks, where they picked up 20 armed policemen. Travelling westwards to Ballincollig RIC Barracks, the convoy picked up four more RIC men but, by the time they reached Berrings it was too dark carry out any searches, and the party returned to Cork.

The operation was repeated on the following morning,

An atmospheric scene in Dublin before the outbreak of the 'Troubles'. Dublin, with its fine Georgian architecture was, at that time, known as 'The Second City of the British Empire'. The Duke of Wellington married Kitty Pakenham in St. George's Church of Ireland church, which can be glimpsed in the background.
Oxfordshire & Buckinghamshire Light Infantry Museum archives

Two views of Fermoy bridge, circa 1895. In September 1919, many Catholic-owned shops and businesses in this normally tranquil town were wrecked by members of the Shropshire Light Infantry in retaliation for an unprovoked attack that had taken place on a party of Methodist soldiers while they were on their way to the local Wesleyan chapel.

Oxfordshire & Buckinghamshire Light Infantry Museum archives

A reminder of happier days in the south of Ireland. Two photographs of Blarney Castle, near Cork, taken by officers of the regiment serving in Ireland during the Victorian era. Ireland, with its ample facilities for hunting and fishing, was a popular posting for members of the 43rd and 52nd regiments – many of whom were themselves Irishmen.

Oxfordshire & Buckinghamshire Light Infantry Museum archives

British troops in Victoria Barracks, Cork, in 1919. It is believed that these photographs were taken during the final parade of the 3rd Battalion, Oxfordshire & Buckinghamshire Light Infantry, which was disembodied on 1st August 1919.

Oxfordshire & Buckinghamshire Light Infantry Museum archives

and the following account from the regimental *Chronicle* is worth quoting in full, insofar as it illustrates the kind of work which would soon become all-too-familiar in the disaffected parts of Ireland:

'We proceeded … by Dripsey to Point 523 on Sheet 186 (Blarney) - a cross roads about half-mile South of Bally Cunningham; here the Police searched two houses and arrested one man, whom we took on to a house about a mile south of Barrabourin, which we searched but found nothing; this was the house of the man who did the shooting (a captain of the Sinn Fein).We then went on foot to a house by Kilmartin Upper which we searched and found a bandolier and water bottle. We arrested a man here and searched another house near by.

One man was seen running away and was chased by a constable and one of our men, but without success, as he had a good start. We then returned to the house we had previously searched and arrested one man in the farm and two men outside, who started to run but were caught. We then had dinners accompanied by the weepings of a dirty old woman, the mother of some of the prisoners.

We were here joined by a 3 ton lorry, which had relieved the broken-down one, and we proceeded with the prisoners to a house between 619 and 533 (on the same road coming back). This we raided but made no arrests, and the party proceeded to the cross roads previously visited, and so to Donoughmore. One house was raided on the way and various illegal documents confiscated. A public house was raided in Donoughmore, and the party then proceeded to a house just north of 3 Cross Roads, Point 438, about one mile south of Garraun North.

One house was raided on the way, and a man arrested who was in bed there. The father (a man of about 70) was considerably annoyed at his house being searched, and tried to fight: two constables and one of his daughters pushed him out with a good deal of effort, and his movements were controlled outside by our party. At the house described (point 436) a certain number of illegal documents and badges were found, the man being a captain of Sinn Fein. After this we returned to Ballincollig and dumped the prisoners there, leaving one light lorry and six police to bring them on to Cork. The party returned to Cork, dropped the police, and arrived in barracks at 17.30 hrs, where teas and dinners were provided'[9].

A few weeks earlier, on Sunday 7th September, there had been an unfortunate incident in the nearby garrison town of Fermoy, when rebels attacked members of the King's Shropshire Light Infantry while they were on their way to the local Wesleyan chapel, 20 year old Private William Jones being killed while several others were injured. Local residents made no attempt to help the injured - the only person brave enough to assist the wounded being the wife of the Wesleyan minister, who took the wounded men into her house and sent for a doctor[10].

Following this unprovoked attack, a party of angry soldiers armed with hammers and iron bars went on a rampage and smashed-up 'between fifty and sixty shops' in the town – hitherto a staunchly loyalist stronghold. It was subsequently decided that the KSLI would be moved from Fermoy to Cork, but this served only to inflame public opinion and, with shootings taking place in the streets of Cork, the Oxfordshire & Buckinghamshire Light Infantry was confined to barracks from 10th November until 18th November 1919, when the King's Shropshire Light Infantry was sent away from Cork to the Curragh[11].

In the early months of 1920, the 1st and 2nd battalions were still stationed at Limerick and Cork respectively, although detachments had been sent out at various times to outlying towns and villages such as Ballincollig and Macroom, to the west of Cork, and Tulla in County Clare, about twenty miles due west from Limerick. Life settled down to a routine of patrols, searches and escort duties, while the men attempted to make themselves comfortable in a variety of premises, including isolated RIC barracks and dilapidated workhouses (most of which had, interestingly, been designed by an Oxfordshire man, William Wilkinson of Witney who had served as architect to the Poor Law Commissioners during the 1840s).

Patrols were carried out on foot, on bicycle or in motor lorries – the most characteristic vehicles in use at that time being Crossley tenders, which were fitted up with outward-facing seats and generally had a crew of one officer and six other ranks. These vehicles had no tailboards or windscreens, and the men travelling in the back of the lorry faced outwards with their Lee-Enfield rifles loaded and ready. Convoys were normally formed of three vehicles, with an interval of at least 200 yards between each lorry. The officer in charge was expected to travel in the rearmost vehicle, while the leading vehicle was equipped a Very pistol which was to be fired in the event of an ambush. As a further precaution against mines and roadside explosives, suspected rebels were sometimes handcuffed to the side of the leading vehicle so that they would take the brunt of any explosion[12].

At one time, road-cutting became so serious that the Royal Engineers supplied planks and large wooden sleepers shaved-down at each end, so that trenches and broken bridges could be safely negotiated. 'Trees and walls built across the road were removed by the simple means of collecting every able-bodied man in the neighbourhood'[13] and making them clear the obstruction. On one occasion, officers of the 1st Battalion ordered their men to commandeer the male worshippers in a Roman Catholic church, but most of the congregation promptly disappeared, leaving a hard and dirty job for just four Catholic civilians in their Sunday best clothes[14]. This was, perhaps, not the best way to win friends and influence people.

Tactical Crossley on duty @ Killaloe — Nenagh
'7-3-21.   *County Clare*

Crossley tenders were widely used by the army and the 'Black & Tans' during the 'Troubles'. This example has been fitted with what appears to be a Lewis gun.   *Oxfordshire & Buckinghamshire Light Infantry Museum archives*

THE AMBUSH AT OOLA

On 26th June 1920 the IRA scored achieved something of a propaganda victory when it captured a Brigadier General while he was on a fishing holiday at Castletownroche, near Fermoy. However, on 31st July *The Times* was able to report that General Lucas had managed to remove the bars from the window of his room and effect an escape. Rain fell in torrents throughout the night and the general had great difficulty in making his way through the fields and hedges but, after further adventures, the intrepid escaper found his way to the safety of Pallas Green RIC Barracks. It was decided that he would be taken to Pallas, from where he could be given a lift on 'the military mail motor from Limerick to Limerick Junction'. Thus, on 30th July 1920, wearing 'civilian clothes and a soft hat', General Lucas boarded a Crossley tender manned by members of the 43rd Light Infantry – the soldiers in the lorry being greatly surprised when they learned the identity of their passenger!

The lorry continued its journey but, at a point about half a mile on the Tipperary side of Oola, and about four miles to the north-west of Limerick Junction, its progress was arrested by a barricade of carts, ladders and a fallen tree. As the vehicle pulled up, a volley was fired by about fifty men who had been waiting in ambush. The soldiers immediately returned fire and, during the fighting, which continued for about half an hour, two soldiers were shot dead and three more wounded, one of them seriously.

While the fight was in progress a second military lorry appeared, followed by six armed policemen from Oola. The ambushing party hastily retreated, and the dead and wounded were taken away in lorries, while the military parties proceeded to Tipperary[15].

It was, at first, thought that the ambush had been staged with the aim of recapturing General Lucas, but contemporary press reports reveal that there was a 'strong rumour in Tipperary that the attackers were not aware that General Lucas was in the military lorry, and that the purpose of the attack was to secure the military mails'. It is interesting to note that John Lynch, a local man from Cappamore in County Limerick, had witnessed the entire incident, and on 31st July 1920 *The Times* printed the following graphic account of the ambush at Oola:

'AN EYE WITNESS'S STORY - I was coming to Tipperary this morning with a cartload of timber in company with my brother Tom. It was about half past nine, and we were about a quarter of a mile on the Tipperary side of Oola, when we heard shots in front of us. We proceeded on our way and a short distance farther on the wife of a farmer named David O'Donnell, ran out in a very excited state on to the road and, putting up her hands, shouted to us not to go any farther, for there was a raid on near Hewitt's Gate. We proceeded on our way, however, and about 30 yards further on a policeman met us, putting up his hands and warning us to stop. We then left the horse and cart

in the middle of the road and went in behind the hedge on the roadside. Looking through the hedge, we saw a motor-lorry some little distance down the road. About a dozen soldiers had got down from the lorry, and were replying with their rifles to shots which came from both sides of the road. Two soldiers lay motionless in the middle of the road, apparently dead. From behind a shed with a corrugated iron roof a heavy and continuous fusillade was directed on the soldiers. I could not say how many men were in the attacking party, but there appeared to be a good number.

When the fight had been in progress about 20 minutes or half an hour, a second motor lorry full of soldiers coming from Limerick raced up to the spot. Following them rushed five or six policemen, rifles in hand. The attackers then dispersed firing as they ran, and the military firing after them. When the fight was over the two dead soldiers, and two or three others, who appeared to be wounded, were placed in the lorry and the two lorries sent on to Tipperary'.

The regimental *Chronicle* subsequently reported that the two men killed in the Oola ambush had been 42797 Lance-Corporal G. B. Parker and 27862 Private Daniel Verey Bayliss of the 1st Battalion, while the injured included privates Snelling, Cornwall and Steer. In an obituary notice, *The Chronicle* recorded that:

'Lance-Corporal Parker was the son of Mr and Mrs Parker of 24 Park Street, High Wycombe; he was only twenty years old at the time of his death, and had eighteen months service, having served with the 43rd in North Russia. Private Bayliss, who was the son of Mrs Bayliss of 7 George Street, St Clements, Oxford, had enlisted in the 43rd Band as a boy at the end of 1916, and was just eighteen when he was killed'[16].

Lance Corporal Parker was buried in High Wycombe Cemetery, while Private Bayliss was interred in Rose Hill Cemetery, Oxford.

INCIDENT AT CRATLOE

At the end of May 1920, rumours began circulating to the effect that the 2nd Battalion were to be sent back to England in order that they could begin preparations for foreign service. The advance party left Cork in June, en route for Lichfield, and the move was complete by 1st July – the 2nd South Staffordshire Regiment being sent from Lichfield to take over at Cork. The officers of the 52nd no doubt left Ireland with mixed feelings, the situation in County Cork being 'not as bad as the daily papers made out'. In fact, they considered that 'Cork City was very well behaved, and no notice was taken of the Military, as the rebels were still concentrating on the Police'[17].

The next major incident involving members of the Oxfordshire & Buckinghamshire Light Infantry took place on 18th November 1920, after an aeroplane had made a forced landing near Punches Quarry at Cratloe in County Clare. The regiment was asked to protect the machine during the night and a platoon from 'C' Company, 1st Battalion was, accordingly, sent out under 2nd Lieutenant M. H. Last. When the party reached Cratloe they apparently set up camp near the aircraft and built themselves a large fire, unaware that a party of IRA men had decided to raid the site to see if they could capture the aeroplane's machine gun. The attackers, led by Joe Clancy of the East Clare brigade, opened fire on the soldiers from an elevated position at about 17.30 hrs, 5373641 Private Alfred Spackman being killed, while 5373574 Private Maurice Robins was severely wounded. The attackers having been driven off, 'C' Company subsequently carried out a 'round up' of known republicans in the Cratloe area[18].

Private Spackman, who had enlisted in the Regiment in April 1920, was the son of Mrs Spackman of Twyford in Berkshire[19]. Private Robins, who never recovered from his wounds, died in Fermoy Hospital on 2nd March 1921. The regimental *Chronicle* reported that he had 'enlisted in the Regiment on 12th February 1920, being just over seventeen years of age. He had previously lived at Wexham, near Slough[20].

One of the most notorious incidents in the rebellion occurred at Kilmichael, near Macroom, on the evening of 28th November 1920 when eighteen members of the RIC Auxiliary Division, travelling in two lorries, were stopped by a man in what appeared to be a British army uniform, who told them that his vehicle had broken down. On going to assist, the patrol drove straight into an ambush, a 'Flying Column' of the 3rd Cork Brigade IRA having been skilfully deployed on both sides of the road by their commander, Thomas Bernadine Barry (1897-1980), a former member of the Royal Artillery. Many of the Auxiliaries were killed by the first volley, the wounded being callously murdered while they lay on the ground[21].

On 1st December 1920, *The Times* reported that most of the bodies had nearly six bullet wounds, and had 'suffered terrible mutilation', as though they had 'been attacked with hatchets'. One man, Cecil Guthrie, an ex-RAF officer from Buckfastleigh in Devon, managed to escape, but he was subsequently captured by the IRA and shot, his body being thrown into a bog (22). Another survivor, H. F. Ford, MC, who was also an ex-RAF man, was found alive at the scene of the ambush, although he had been shot in the head and was brain damaged.

The bodies of the murdered Auxiliaries were subsequently conveyed to Fishguard aboard the destroyer HMS *Undine*, prior to which they had passed through the streets of Cork with full military ceremony, shops and business premises having been closed for the day, while the inhabitants of the City, whether loyalists or rebel supporters, stood with bared heads as the bodies passed – those who refused to remove their hats having them knocked off and stamped on by the police or soldiers.

MUTILATED BODIES.

An official report issued from Dublin Castle last night states that the bodies of the 16 murdered men will be conveyed in a destroyer to Fishguard, accompanied by an escort of police auxiliaries. The bodies will pass with military ceremony through Cork. Inspection has revealed that the bodies have nearly all six bullet wounds, and have suffered terrible mutilation, as though they had been hacked with hatchets. No trace has been found of the missing cadet.

The following is an official list of the casualties :—

KILLED.

Captain F. W. CRAKE, M.C. (late Bedford Regiment), 57, Stanton-street, Newcastle-on-Tyne.

Captain P. N. GRAHAM (late Northumberland Fusiliers), 14, Wootton-road, Abingdon, Berks.

Major F. HUGO, O.B.E., M.C. (late Indian Army), Grove House, Southgate, N.

Captain W. PALLESTER (late R.A.F.), care of Mrs. Brooke, 71, Primrose-avenue, Shire Green, Sheffield.

Captain C. WAINWRIGHT (late Royal Dublin Fusiliers), 13, Brunswick-road, Gravesend.

Cadet W. T. BARNES, D.F.C. (late R.A.F.), 47, Glebe-road, Sutton, Surrey.

Cadet L. D. BRADSHAW (late R.F.A.), 34, Larkhill-terrace, Blackburn.

Cadet J. C. GLEAVE (late R.A.F.), Crowdale, Canterbury.

Cadet A. G. JONES (late Suffolk Regiment), 56, Swindon-road, Wroughton, Wilts.

Cadet W. Hooper JONES (late Northumberland Fusiliers), Mount Pleasant, Hawkstone, Tottington, Bury, Lancs.

Cadet E. W. H. LUCAS (late Sussex Regiment), Terringes, West Tarring, Worthing.

Cadet H. O. PEARSON (Yorkshire Regiment), 22, St. Paul's-square, York.

Cadet F. TAYLOR (late R.A.F.), 21, Seaview-road, Gillingham, Kent.

Cadet B. WEBSTER (late 8th Black Watch), 300, Langside-road, Crosshill, Glasgow.

Temporary Cadet C. D. W. BAYLEY (late R.A.F.), 24, Reynard-road, Chorlton-cum-Hardy, Manchester.

Temporary Constable A. F. POOLE (late Royal West Kent Regiment), 35, Rodney-street, Pentonville-road, N.

Sixteen victims of the Kilmichael Massacre were listed in *The Times* on 1st December 1920, although Cecil Guthrie, the seventeenth victim who was still missing, was not included. Captain Graham, formerly of the Northumberland Fusiliers, is buried in a war grave in Abingdon Cemetery.

THE DROMKEEN AMBUSH

The 'Kilmichael Massacre' coincided with an alarming escalation in the IRA terror campaign and, in consequence, attitudes began to harden on both sides. In November 1920 the 1st Battalion officers in Limerick were ordered to live either in barracks or at Cruise's Hotel, while in the following month Martial Law was declared throughout the troubled counties of Cork, Limerick, Kerry and Tipperary. As an added precaution, officers were ordered to carry side arms and told never to go out alone[23].

On 3rd February 1921 the IRA ambushed two police vehicles at a place called Dromkeen, on the road from Caherconlish to Pallas Green in County Limerick. The attack, which began at about 14.30 hrs, caused the first lorry to crash into a wall, leaving its occupants either dead or injured by the roadside. The second vehicle then came under intense fire before the RIC men could respond to the situation. Eleven policemen were killed in the Dromkeen Ambush, three of them being shot after they had surrendered. The murdered RIC men included constables Samuel Adams, George Bell, John Bourke, Michael Doyle, Patrick Foody, William Hayton, William Kingston, Sidney Millin, Bernard Mollaghan, Arthur Pearce and Henry Smith.

The Dromkeen Ambush was particularly significant in that, on this occasion, the authorities sanctioned a policy of 'official reprisals'. Accordingly, on 4th February 1921, the First Battalion Diary recorded that 'six officers and 60 other ranks were engaged in burning houses in an official reprisal for a very serious ambush of police at Dromkeen'[24]. As a result of this action about ten houses were burnt, all of these being the homes of known or suspected IRA men. This deeply controversial measure was, in effect, a reversion to the tactics that had been used against the Boers in South Africa – the idea being that the insurgents would be denied access to food and shelter. In response, the IRA started burning the country houses of prominent Irish Protestants – particularly in the province of Munster, where the wanton destruction of Ireland's artistic and architectural heritage was particularly severe.

As a corollary of its policy of reprisals and house-burning, the government introduced a programme of 'great drives' whereby large areas of open countryside were methodically searched for rebels. Between 5th and 10th June 1921, for example, members of the 17th Lancers, the 93rd Highlanders, the 43rd, and the Auxiliary Division carried out a 'Sinn Fein Drive' in County Clare. Cottages in the designated search area were entered, each producing 'its male or males to be handed over, at the end of the drive, the Intelligence Officer' – although it seems unlikely that these unfortunate people would actually have been rebels. At length, an RIC man at Feakle reported that Coolregh Bog, which was surrounded by broken, or 'knocked' bridges, was being used by the IRA as a hide-out:

'The bog lay in a triangle formed by three roads, all of which had been "knocked" at the angles or apices of the triangle. The 93rd Highlanders took the eastern, the Auxiliaries the northern angle, while the 43rd started at the southern, intending to drive NE. The plan was completely successful, the three companies arriving at their positions practically simultaneously, and by three different roads. At first the 43rd were completely baulked by a very broad river, which ran along the side of the bog. It seemed un-crossable, and yet the bog was well represented by turf-cutters, who on sight of the "Militthary" immediately downed tools and started to make shift in case of music.

For a distance of a mile the 43rd walked up the side of the river until at last they found a narrow causeway leading across. The leading platoon crossed and deployed, facing practically due east, and moved forward. Sergeant Bristow topped a bank in front of him, and dropped down the other side and, being no light weight, fell through the roof of a dug-out. As a ferret bolts a rabbit, so did three Sinn Feiners bolt out and make away across the bog. The 43rd opened fire, the "Shinners" carried on, scuttling among the turf piles, making straight for the 93rd. Suddenly the music of Lewis guns rang out; they had done exactly as had been intended. Straight into the mouthpiece of the inhospitable little weapon did these beauties run.

The bog was driven, and every male taken, in all 250 odd. They could not get out, they were surrounded and helpless. Accordingly this little party was formed up and proceeded at a smart double to Feakle. It was a hot day, and Feakle was two and a half miles away, the road was uphill all the way, but not a single Hibernian fell out. At Feakle the police singled out five men, all of whom were on the black list for murder, and these were handcuffed and taken back to camp'[25].

In parenthesis, it may be pertinent to ask how the army was able to differentiate between rebel supporters and loyalists, and although captured documents and intelligence material among the Oxfordshire & Buckinghamshire Light Infantry archival collections suggest that a great deal was known about the organisation, methods and membership of the IRA, there remains a very strong suspicion that ordinary, working class Irish Catholics were regarded, without distinction, as rebel supporters. On the other hand the Protestants, who tended to belong to the upper and middle classes, were assumed to be staunch allies. An officer of the 43rd recalled that 'many local friendships were formed' – for instance 'one very loyal old lady sent up a bottle of priceless old brown sherry for the officers and a bundle of books for the sentry to read'. Indeed, the officers admitted that the army and police were 'wholeheartedly assisted by our friends the Irish Loyalists';

'For their hospitality and kindness we cannot thank them enough. Consisting as they did of people with everything to gain and nothing to lose by preserving an attitude of neutrality; in constant danger of seeing their houses burned and their motor cars purloined, even if they escaped actual physical violence; they continued to invite us to dances and tennis parties, and do everything possible for our entertainment. Their courage was undoubted, but for any influence they had on the opinions and actions of the population as whole (even their own employees) they might just as well have been living in another country. Indeed their absence would have made our task more easy. Their number and situation made the provision of any kind of protection extremely difficult. They were hostages in the hands of the enemy, a fact the Sinn Feiners were quick to realise'[26].

It should be added that, although most Roman Catholics in the south of Ireland were probably Home Rule supporters they did not necessarily condone the use of violence; for instance, the officers of the 1st Battalion were slightly perplexed by 'one old priest' who would walk into the Orderly Room in Limerick and talk 'rapidly and painfully on the situation in general'. On one occasion he produced 'a handful of raisins from his pocket' and poured them onto the desks of the Commanding Officer and Adjutant, presumably as a token of friendship[27].

SOLDIERS MURDERED AT WOODFORD

In retrospect, the first six months of 1921 were perhaps the worst period of the 'Black & Tan' rebellion, the IRA campaign of murder and intimidation being at its peak. The victims were, in many cases, policemen, although off-duty soldiers and Protestants were also regarded as legitimate targets on the pretext that they were 'spies' or 'traitors'. On 22nd February 1921 three members of the regiment, 5374617 Private H. Morgan, 5374675, Private W. S. Walker and 5373002, Private David John Williams, were found murdered by rebels near Woodford in County Galway. They had been reported missing from Strand Barracks on 13th February, and nothing more was heard of them until their dead bodies were found by a farmer at Woodford. The IRA had placed the following message around the neck of one of their victims: 'Spies. Tried by Court Martial and found Guilty. Let all others beware.'

Their bodies were brought into Limerick, and subsequently sent to England for burial. The regimental *Chronicle* subsequently reported that Private Morgan had enlisted into the Regiment on 23rd May 1919, having previously served in the Labour Corps during World War I. Private Walker, whose home was near Bicester, had re-enlisted into the Regiment after wartime service on 5th August 1919; he was twenty-three years of age at the time of his death. Private Williams was, similarly, a veteran of the Great War who had served for about fourteen years in the Gloucestershire Regiment and re-enlisted into the Oxfordshire & Buckinghamshire Light Infantry on 4th December 1919; he was thirty-three years old when he was killed[28].

On 11th April 1921 *The Times* reported that a bomb which had been thrown in the city of Limerick on Friday night near the John Street Police barracks had killed an elderly man named Francis McMahon and wounded several other persons. Shots were also fired at an RIC patrol from a lane, and a head constable, two sergeants, and a constable were dangerously wounded. The military arrived soon afterwards and some arrests were made. On Friday two police constables stationed at Carrigdrohid, County Cork, obtained eight hours leave and spent the day in the neighbouring town of Macroom. On returning to their station in the afternoon they borrowed a horse and trap, but when they reached a place named Manchinaglass they were ambushed by about a dozen men, Constable Frederick Lord being instantly killed, although his companion was able to escape.

In response to the Limerick bomb attack and other outrages, the Oxfordshire & Buckinghamshire Light Infantry was again ordered to carry out official reprisals in Limerick, several rebel houses being burned, while 'one hundred other ranks of the regiment furnished patrols and piquets for this area'. Local people still recall the ensuing destruction, the consensus of opinion being that the regiment had wreaked unnecessary havoc – although there is no doubt that the reprisal was officially-sanctioned. It is unclear what opinions the rank-and-file may have harboured about the policy of official reprisals, though it may be significant that six officers of the 43rd Light Infantry resigned their commissions between 16th April and 19th July 1921.

MURDER OF A BARONET'S DAUGHTER
On Saturday 14th May 1921, Lieutenant W. T. Trengrouse, an officer of the 1st Battalion, was involved in an ambush while motoring between Glenstal and Newport in company with District Inspector Major Harry Biggs of the RIC, and Miss Winifred Barrington, the only daughter of Sir Charles and Lady Barrington of Glenstal Castle. The party also included a young lady named Miss Coverdale and Captain William Gabbett, a friend of the Barrington family. On reaching Coolboreen Bridge near Newport, in County Tipperary, the motor car was fired at by a party of armed men led by Sean Gaynor, Miss Barrington and the district inspector being fatally wounded, while Captain Gabbett surrendered and Lieutenant Trengrouse managed to escape from the vehicle and run down the road. Witnesses later reported that Major Biggs was shot 'ten or twelve times' while he was lying injured in the roadway, though one of the IRA gunmen 'then went back to the motor car where Miss Barrington was lying and said something about being sorry'[29].

This appalling crime was just one incident in a catalogue of murders which were carried out by the IRA in the south and west of Ireland over the weekend of 14th and 15th May 1921. In Tralee, for instance, Head Constable Francis Benson was shot and mortally wounded a few yards from his front door, while as a result of two bombs thrown at a police patrol in Cork City, Constable Coughlan was killed and several other RIC men were severely injured. Patrick Sheehan, a cattle dealer, was shot dead at Cork in the presence of his wife by armed and disguised men and Constable Thomas Bridges was shot dead while shopping at Drumcollegher on Saturday night.

Private Francis William Sheppard of the Essex Regiment, who was one of an armed guard protecting a party of military and police who were playing a football match at Bandon, was shot dead, and a civilian named Looney was fatally wounded. Three unarmed soldiers were shot dead on the pier at Castletown, Berehaven, by armed men in civilian dress and other soldiers were shot dead at Bandon and Courtmacsherry, County Cork. Police Sergeant Joseph Coleman was shot dead in a public house at Midleton, County Cork, and Constables Thomas Cornyn and Harold Thompson were cruelly murdered while trying to find a priest to attend their dying colleague. In another incident, Constable John Kenna was shot dead by four gunmen in a field near his barracks at Innishannon, County Cork.

THE TULLA AMBUSH
The next major incident involving members of the Oxfordshire & Buckinghamshire Light Infantry occurred near Tulla on the morning of 28th June 1921 when a patrol consisting of twenty-two year-old Lieutenant Richard Crawford Warren MC and eleven men was ambushed on their way back to Tulla Workhouse at about 2.00 am. The patrol, which had been sent out to prevent the rebels from felling trees across the roads, was approaching Fortaine cross roads when a civilian suddenly appeared in the middle of the road. Lieutenant Warren went forward to speak to the impassive figure, but at that moment the man drew a revolver from his pocket and shot the officer in the stomach at more or less point blank range. The rebels immediately opened fire from both sides of the road, most of the fire coming from the right. Two more soldiers were wounded but, taking charge of the situation, Sergeant Thomas Swift rallied his men and mounted a spirited counter-attack, at which point the rebels fled from the scene[30].

Lieutenant Richard Warren MC, shot by the IRA on 28th June 1921.
Oxfordshire & Buckinghamshire Light Infantry Museum

This message, marked 'very urgent', was sent to Tulla by carrier pigeon after Lieutenant Warren had been shot in the stomach at point blank range.

Oxfordshire & Buckinghamshire Light Infantry Museum archives

Meanwhile, it was clear that Lieutenant Warren had been severely injured, and he died of his wounds at 21.30 hrs. On 1st July the body of the murdered officer was placed on a gun carriage and escorted to Limerick railway station 'by the whole Regiment and by representatives of the garrison and the RIC of Limerick and Tulla'. He was buried in Brookwood Cemetery on 5th July 1921. Lieutenant Warren, a former pupil of Gresham's School in Norfolk who had been wounded twice during the Great War, had been awarded the Military Cross and bar for conspicuous gallantry during that conflict. Having survived the horrors of the Western Front it was particularly tragic that his life should have ended on a quiet country road amid the beautiful countryside of County Clare.

In addition to the members of the 43rd Light Infantry who were killed as a direct result of rebel activity, the 1st Battalion lost a small number of men as a result or road accidents or other mishaps, one of the most unfortunate incidents being that which involved 5373689 Lance-Corporal M. Hudson of 'D' Company, who was accidentally killed while on a bicycle patrol at Tulla on 12th June 1921. It appears that a routine patrol had been sent out from their base at the Workhouse to round up any suspected rebels or other suspicious characters who might be met with but, on returning through Tulla, a nervous sentry at the RIC Barracks assumed that the patrol was a gang of rebels and opened fire, killing Lance-Corporal Hudson. The dead man, a Londoner, had re-enlisted in the Regiment on 5th May 1920 after four years previous service[31].

A report of the Tulla Ambush made out by Sergeant Thomas Swift, who led the counter-attack after Lieutenant Warren had been shot.

Oxfordshire & Buckinghamshire Light Infantry Museum archives

A detailed sketch map, prepared by Sergeant Swift to accompany his written report. Thomas Swift, a native of Southall in Middlesex, was a veteran of the Great War who had survived brutal treatment at the hands of the Turks. A recipient of the DCM, he had also served in Russia in 1919. On 7th January 1922 he married Catherine Cronin at Limerick and subsequently had three daughters – Kathleen, Barbara and Jean. He left the army in 1929.

Oxfordshire & Buckinghamshire Light Infantry Museum archives

to Bodyke

N. (approx)

Cottage

Scrub

grass field

B

Open grass field

Copse

to Tulla

0   50   100   approx.

Sketch of ambush at 0230 hrs Fortane Cross Rds (28.6.21) All the roads have stone walls about 4½' high.

Position of patrol when civilian appeared at point X

Patrol first fired on from points A & B (only slightly from the latter)

Route taken by Patrol. When getting over the wall at C patrol was fired on from behind wall at D so took up the position ——↑—— & fired North down the line of trees.

THE ANGLO-IRISH TRUCE

A 43rd officer later declared that 'on looking back, June 1921 was the deciding month in the Irish War'. Martial law had been in force in the south and south-western counties for a period of six months and, towards the end of May, 'it seemed that a condition of stalemate had been reached between the Crown Forces and the rebels'. Although the rebel outrages did not increase, the captures made by the Crown Forces of militant rebels had increased, with the result that the IRA 'Active Service Companies' and 'Flying Columns' had become smaller and less well organized as the weeks went by.

The general feeling among the Oxfordshire & Buckinghamshire Light Infantry officers was that the rebels were on the verge of defeat. It was felt that, for once, 'the Government were going to take a really strong hand' and smash the rebels once and for all; in modern parlance, Lloyd George was about to order a 'surge' in Southern Ireland. In June 1921 the 2nd Battalion were ordered back to Ireland, an advance party of two officers and 20 other ranks reaching Tipperary on 27th June, while sixteen officers and 420 other ranks left Lichfield on 30th June and arrived at Queenstown in the early hours of 2nd July. As the rebels had started attacking troop trains and sabotaging the Irish railway system, the Battalion travelled from Queenstown to Tipperary in two special trains, each of which was preceded by a pilot engine and escorted by an aeroplane[32].

It was envisaged that the 2nd Battalion would reinforce the Green Howards and the Lincolnshire Regiment, 'A' and 'C' companies being stationed in Tipperary while 'B' and 'D' companies would be based in Cashel and Fethard respectively. However, by mid-1921, it was clear that public opinion in Britain (and indeed throughout the entire English-speaking world) had become deeply divided over the question of Ireland. In particular, the Labour and Liberal parties had become so concerned at the allegedly brutal activities of the Black & Tans that the British government was obliged to moderate its earlier position of outright opposition to Irish home rule. In May 1921 Lord FitzAlan had become the very first Roman Catholic Viceroy in Dublin, while later that year King George V made a compassionate and conciliatory speech at the opening of the first elected Ulster Parliament. A 'truce' was declared shortly afterwards, on 11th July 1921.

It has been estimated that around 1,000 people had been killed during the 'Black & Tan rebellion', most of the victims being members of the Royal Irish Constabulary, IRA men or innocent civilians. The regular army, which had played very little part in the fighting, lost 146 men, whereas the RIC lost around 560 men as a result of terrorist activity between 1916 and 1922.

THE CIVIL WAR PERIOD

In 1921, a treaty culminated in the creation of 'The Irish Free State' as a self-governing dominion within the British Empire, and twenty-six mainly Catholic Irish counties thereby seceded from the United Kingdom, leaving six predominantly Protestant Ulster counties within the Union. The treaty provided that the harbour defences and port facilities at Berehaven, Cork, Lough Swilly and Belfast Lough would remain under the control of the British government, which would retain overall responsibility for the defence of Ireland against external attack.

Sadly, many hard-line members of the IRA refused to accept peace on these compromise terms, and by 1922 there were renewed hostilities between the extreme republicans and the newly-created Irish Free State Army. It is generally considered that The Irish Civil War began on 28th June 1922, when the Free State Army began bombarding the Dublin law Courts – the Four Courts – which had been occupied by members of the IRA. The rebels surrendered two days later, after they had detonated a large mine which had been placed in the Irish Record Office – the destruction of the Irish Public Records in this massive explosion being an act of unforgivable vandalism.

This remarkable photograph, which was presumably taken from the North Dublin Union Workhouse, shows the massive explosion which destroyed the Four Courts and thereby obliterated many thousands of official documents – an event which has caused immense problems for family historians. It is said that up to twelve mines were laid, but the IRA managed to detonate only one of them.

Oxfordshire & Buckinghamshire Light Infantry Museum archives

A newspaper advertisement asking for ex-British officers with 'first class records' to join the RIC Auxiliary Division, 'courage, discretion, tact and judgment' being among the qualities required.

Perhaps surprisingly, the Oxfordshire & Buckinghamshire Light Infantry were present in Dublin while these momentous events were taking place, the 1st Battalion having moved from Limerick to Dublin in the early part of 1922, their new home being the North Dublin Union workhouse as the Curragh, Beggar's Bush and most of the other former British army barracks had been handed over to the Free State in compliance with the terms of the treaty. This gloomy edifice provided a grandstand view of the attack on the Four Courts, as recorded in the following extract from the regimental *Chronicle*:

'Our next move was to the North Dublin Union, which the 1st Battalion of the Lancashire Fusiliers had been occupying for some time. Standing, as it does, well above the surrounding houses, the North Dublin Union can be recommended to visitors to Dublin as a most suitable position from which to view any fracas that may be going on at the time. We found it excellent for this purpose, and during the whole of the so-called Battle of the Four Courts, the windows and fire escapes were thronged with sightseers.

This battle was perhaps the most humorous of the many humorous incidents which we witnessed in Ireland. The Republican bravoes, under the leadership of one Rory O'Connor, had seized the Four Courts. This was understood to be a silent protest against the Free State Party for keeping to themselves all the barracks handed over by the British Government, such conduct being considered a gross breach of etiquette towards old comrades, whose watchword in their joint enterprises in the past had always been Fifty-fifty.

They barricaded the windows with record books and title deeds, of which they found a good supply. When asked to return these valuable documents to their proper place, they answered that they would be unable to do so, unless issued with sandbags in lieu. All these records were subsequently destroyed. For some time they continued to live there unmolested, without doing much harm to anybody except the local shopkeepers, from whom they purchased large supplies of food, putting the same down to the account of Mr De Valera, whose credit at that time was not very high. However, the day arrived when the Free State authorities decided that this nuisance had existed long enough. The artillery were ordered to bring up their gun, and the bombardment of the Four Courts began. The gun, an eighteen pounder it was stated on the best authority, was fired by a Colonel of the Free State Army, who aimed it by taking out the breech-block and peering down the barrel. In order to avoid unnecessary loss of life, the method employed was to train the gun on a certain part of the building for a minute or two, to allow the occupants to move away from

Alarming news from Ireland, as reported in *The Times* on 11th April 1921.

the part threatened. A round would then be fired, the gun laid on a new target, and the defenders would move back to their original position, which, although a little draughty, would be safe for the next few hours.

At the end of the first day, the Commander of the Irregulars, who had suffered no casualties, issued an order of the day to his supporters, in which, after comparing the defence of the Four Courts to that of Verdun, he finished up with the stirring words "Father Dominie is with us, the boys are glorious". The Commander of the Free State Troops, who had also fortunately escaped without loss, contented himself with saying if his men continued to show such fortitude in the face of dangers and hardships hitherto imagined, victory was assured.

On the third day the Four Courts were reduced. The "glorious boys", such of them as had escaped through the back door, were shepherded into captivity at Kilmainham Gaol, and contest resolved itself into a running fight up and down Dublin, culminating in the destruction large part of Sackville Street. This part of the city seems fated to be unlucky; it was badly smashed up in 1916.

Apart from the view it affords of Dublin, the North Dublin Union cannot be commended as a place of residence. Of the Irish workhouse in which we dwelt, it was probably the worst; the walls were black, the accommodation cramped and the whole atmosphere of the place mouldy in the extreme. For all that we managed to spend quite a pleasant summer there. Training was done in Phoenix Park, companies going into camp there for a week at a time. The ground of the lunatic asylum, which lay just behind the North Dublin Union, was at our disposal on two or three days a week for cricket, and we had many good matches there, and also in Phoenix Park'.

Having driven the IRA out of Dublin, the Free State government was obliged to use its army to hunt down the hard-core rebels. At its peak, the Free State 'National Army' was about 60,000 strong, and having raised this new force, the Free State government had no hesitation in imposing a military solution in the disaffected districts, the rebels being, in many cases, shot out of hand (also thrown down wells, run-over by armoured cars or forced to walk over their own mines). This stage of the Irish conflict was, moreover, marred by an upsurge in sectarian murders in both parts of Ireland. For example, fifteen Protestants, many of them elderly people, were shot in their own homes around Bandon, Dunmanway and Drimoleague in April 1922. The victims included the Rev Ralph Harbord, son of the Rector of Murragh, who was shot on the doorstep of his father's Rectory.

The Irish Civil War was a disastrous period for Ireland insofar as immense damage was caused to the railway system and to many of Ireland's finest buildings. The extreme republicans had always viewed railways, public buildings and great country houses as 'soft' targets for their campaign of terror and sabotage, one of the most spectacular acts of destruction being the blowing up of

the 'Ten Arch Bridge' at Mallow on 8th August 1922. This act of wanton destruction severed the Dublin to Cork main line with the result that Cork became cut off from the rest of the Irish railway system.

The Free State suffered a major blow on 22nd August 1922 when Michael Collins, a former IRA commander who had become the commander-in-chief of the Free State Army, was shot dead in an IRA ambush at Bealnablath, between Bandon and Macroom, while riding in an open motor car. The tragic death of General Collins stunned and shocked all Ireland, and *The Cork Examiner* referred to the 'appalling catastrophe that had befallen the Irish people'.

Meanwhile, the long association between Southern Ireland and the 43rd and 52nd regiments was coming to an end Oxfords. It was clear that, by 1922, the IRA had been defeated, the Free Staters having driven the irregulars into hiding. Accordingly, the 2nd Battalion left Tipperary, en route for England, on 20th January 1922[33], while the 1st Battalion sailed from Dublin North Wall for the last time at 15.50 hrs on 14th September 1922[34]. Hostilities between Free State Forces and the IRA dragged on, in desultory

GEN. LUCAS'S ADVENTURES.

(FROM OUR SPECIAL CORRESPONDENT.)

DUBLIN, Aug. 4.

The first news of the adventures of General Lucas which has any claim to authenticity reached Dublin this afternoon. An inquiry into his capture has been concluded in Ireland, but no details have been made public. It is, however, certain that General Lucas was not confined in the same place for more than three or four days together. He was guarded night and day by either a brigade or battalion commandant of the Irish Volunteers. His treatment was absolutely correct in accordance with the rules of war for an officer of his rank. On the last night of his incarceration these officers, however, had left their post in order to organize the attack on the mail lorry which was ambushed at Oola. This was a sheer coincidence. General Lucas in their absence found no difficulty in removing the bars of his prison. He believes that most of his custodians were deportees from among the Republicans who were imprisoned at Wormwood-scrubs.

After a rest and recuperation at the barracks at Pallas he was conveyed on the mail lorry to Tipperary. During the fight at Oola he was as busy as the privates of the military party with a rifle, and in his efforts to counter the attack of the raiding party he received two slight wounds, one under the nose and another in the forehead.

RAILWAY TRACK WRECKED.

The line on the Burtonport Railway (Co. Donegal) at two points, one near Crolly and the other at a deep ravine near Letterkenny, was completely wrecked yesterday. Two hundred and forty yards of rails were torn up and thrown into the lake, together with the sleepers, and in the ravine many tons of granite blasted from the mountain side overwhelmed the track with *débris* so completely that the railway authorities say it will take months to relay the line.

ENGLISH RECRUITS FOR R.I.C.

One hundred and thirty English recruits for the R.I.C. arrived in Dublin yesterday.

An extract from *The Times* dated 5th August 1920, reporting the escape of General Lucas, an attack on the County Donegal Railway and the arrival of 130 English police recruits.

fashion, until 23rd May 1923, by which time around 4,000 people had been killed in the civil war, and the 'Black and Tan' rebellion that had preceded it.

MAJOR CROSS IN NORTHERN IRELAND

The 'official departure' from the 26 counties was not by any means the end of the regiment's long association with Ireland, because at least one officer (himself of Irish descent) was seconded to the Government of Northern Ireland in an intelligence role. Having crossed from Fleetwood on 4th July 1922 aboard the London & North Western Railway steamer *Duke of Connaught* to take up his new post as one of six 'County Intelligence Officers', Bt Major R.B.Crosse (as he then was) arrived in Belfast on the following morning, his initial impression being that the beleaguered city was still on a war footing. He recalled that:

'Belfast reminded me of Ypres as we knew it in November, 1914, many places of business being barricaded, and armed constables standing sentry over many other buildings, especially the banks, the General Post Office, the Royal Avenue Hotel, and, of course, the headquarters of the Constabulary and the Military Adviser's Staff. Here and there were traces of damage due to what insurance policies call "Rebellion, Insurrection, Riot or Civil Commotion." Occasionally an armoured car or "cage" would go by, and altogether the city had a very bellicose appearance which contrasted strangely with my late surroundings, but it gave promise of a life far more interesting. I think what struck me most was the great number of armed police in the streets, and, in fact, wherever one went, and I wondered how much all this would cost, and who would pay for it'.[35]

At this juncture, it should be mentioned that, although Northern Ireland had been spared the worst excesses of the 1919-21 Black & Tan campaign, the RIC had, nevertheless, been kept fully occupied by outbursts of vicious rioting and sectarian murder that erupted from 1920 onwards between rival groups of Catholics and Protestants. There was, moreover, constant trouble along the Irish border, with serious disturbances at Belleek, Pettigo and other places. In the meantime, The Royal Irish Constabulary had been disbanded, its final parade having been held in Pheonix Park on 22nd April. However, in Northern Ireland, a new force known as 'The Royal Ulster Constabulary' was created on 1st June 1922 – this new organisation being, from its inception, an armed police force, its 3,000 regulars being supported by three categories of 'Specials'.

This much-expanded police force had more or less won its battle against the IRA by the summer of 1922, and Lieut-Colonel Cross began to feel that he was, 'comparatively speaking, unemployed'. At length an occupation was found for him which afforded 'the opportunity of visiting almost every town and village in the counties of Derry, Fermanagh, Tyrone, Armagh, Antrim and Down'. In this capacity, he evidently made several intelligence-gathering visits to the south, apparently disguised as an IRA 'irregular'. This led to an amusing incident on 23rd August 1922 when a burst tyre had prevented an immediate return to Northern Ireland, and Lt-Col Cross was approached by a talkative old man who kept a wayside spirit store. Fortunately, the British officers were good actors and, as Cross later recalled:

'It was a complement to the way we had obeyed are orders to adopt a disreputable appearance that he mistook us for the wrong side, whispering to me as we moved on "Put your gun out of sight, sonny, ye'll find the milithary terrible watchful further on". I found that a revolver was showing out of my coat pocket'.

Having resumed their journey, the next obstacle was the re-entry into Northern Ireland, the heavily-sandbagged border town of Pettigo being defended by:

'A picket of the North Staffordshire Regiment. They were all young soldiers, and the zeal with which, as we came from the Free State, they hemmed us in with bayonets while we got out our passes was delightful. From here we took the road via Kesh, Ederney and Lack, stopping on the way to watch a parade of B Specials. Finding that the instructor was an old rifleman, I commented on his teaching them to slope arms. He said the rifles were safer pointing in the air'.[36]

In the course of his perambulations around the northern counties of Ireland, Lieut-Colonel Cross also passed through Maghera, in County Londonderry on the road between Toome and Dungiven. This was the birthplace of Bugler Robert Hawthorne, who had won the Victoria Cross during the Indian Mutiny – though it was mistakenly called 'Moghera' in the Historical Record of the 52nd. Lt-Colonel Crosse made inquiries to ascertain if any of his family were still be there, 'having visions of recruiting another for the Regiment'.

On another occasion, the Lieut-Colonel was able to visit the home of his ancestor John Cross, who had served in the 52nd Light Infantry between 1805 and 1831. His house in County Armagh had recently come into the possession of 'a gentleman who … was in Belfast gaol; and it was burnt down six months later'. In the Church at Killylea, close to it, was a marble tablet, 'having at the top the Colours of the 52nd, with two buglers as supporters', and below is this inscription:

Sacred to the Memory of
LIEUT-COLONEL JOHN CROSS, K.H.
Born January 17, 1787. Died September 27 1850
Son of the late William Cross, of Dartan
(twenty years a Deputy-Governor of this County)
Colonel Cross was a member of the Royal
Hanoverian Guelphic Order,
Sometime Lieut-Governor of Jamaica and
a Magistrate of this County.

APPENDIX 1: MEMBERS OF THE REGIMENT KILLED IN IRELAND 1919-1921

Name	Number	Date of Death	Place of Death
Private Daniel V. Bayliss	27862	30-07-1920	Oola
Lance-Corporal G. B. Parker	47297	30-07-1920	Oola
Private Alfred Spackman	5373641	18-11-1920	Cratloe
Private H. Morgan	5374617	22-02-1921	Woodford
Private W. S. Walker	5374675	22-02-1921	Woodford
Private David J. Williams	5373002	22-02-1921	Woodford
Private Maurice Robins	5373574	02-03-1921	Fermoy Hospital
Lance-Corporal M. Hudson	5373689	12-06-1921	Tulla
Lieutenant Richard C. Warren MC		28-06-1921	Limerick Hospital

APPENDIX 2: MEMBERS OF THE REGIMENT KILLED BY ACCIDENT OR ILLNESS

Name	Number	Date	Place
Private Joseph Baker	23801	01-05-1920	Victoria Barracks Cork
Private Alfred Stonnell	9700	04-08-1920	Limerick Workhouse
Bugle Boy Stanley Pegler	5373974	18-08-1920	Limerick Hospital
Private A. Williams	5373728	01-01-1921	Ballyvonare
Private F. C. Curtis	5373986	03-02-1921	Nenagh
Private Walter Wiggins*	5373116	05-03-1921	Limerick
Private George Fordham	5373745	24-09-1921	Dublin

Wiggins was also known as Walter Jones. He died of a 'self-inflicted wound'.

SOURCES & FOOTNOTES

1 Rowse, A.L. *The Expansion of Elizabethan England* (1955).

2 Ulster's Solemn League & Covenant, 28th September 1912.

3 Fergusson, Sir James, *The Curragh Incident* (1964), *passim*.

4 Duff, Charles, *Six Days to Shake an Empire*, *passim*.

5 Bennett, Richard, *The Black & Tans*

6 The Regimental *Chronicle* 1919-20 p.59.

7 *Ibid.*, pps.156-159.

8 *Ibid.*, p.134.

9 *Ibid.*,

10 *The Times*, 9th September 1919.

11 The Regimental *Chronicle* 1919-20 p.142.

12 The Regimental *Chronicle* 1921 p.68.

13 *Ibid.*

14 The Regimental *Chronicle* 1922

15 *The Times* 31st July 1920.

16 The Regimental *Chronicle* 1919-20, pps.162 & 202-203.

17 *Ibid.*, p.165.

18 *Ibid.*, p.163.

19 *Ibid.*, p.203

20 The Regimental *Chronicle* 1921, p.206.

21 *The Times*, 1st December 1920.

22 In 1926 The Irish Free State Minister of Home Affairs interceded with the IRA on behalf of the Guthrie family, and the missing man's remains were disinterred and handed into the care of the Church of Ireland authorities at Macroom for Christian burial.

23 The Regimental *Chronicle* 1919-20, pps.163-164.

24 The Regimental *Chronicle* 1921, p.13.

25 The Regimental *Chronicle* 1922 pps.130-143.

26 *Ibid.*, p.148.

27 The Regimental *Chronicle* 1921, p.67-68.

28 *Ibid.*, pps.13 & 207.

29 *The Times*, 16th May 1920. See also Hannan, Kevin, Tragedy at Coolboreen, *The Old Limerick Journal*.

30 The Regimental *Chronicle* 1921, pps. 16-17 & 203-206.

31 *Ibid.*, p.207.

32 *Ibid.*, pps. 21 & 72-73.

33 The Regimental *Chronicle*, p.54.

34 *Ibid.*, pps.47-48.

35 Crosse, Lt-Col R.B., Six Months in Northern Ireland, The Regimental *Chronicle* 1923, pps.152-164.

36 *Ibid.*

THE 52nd LIGHT INFANTRY IN PALESTINE

Colonel P. E. Gerahty CBE

On 18th-19th May 1945 the 52nd returned to Bulford Camp, in Wiltshire, from its final location during World War II at Bad Kleinen near the Baltic Sea, which had been reached just prior to VE Day. It was despatched immediately on 14 days bloc leave. Shortly after its return, the Regiment received three orders:- firstly, to prepare to move with the rest of the 6th Airborne Division to SE Asia Command in the early autumn, for an operation which popular rumour said was to be in French Indo-China (though later evidence suggested that the likely objective was the Japanese mainland); secondly, to be prepared to send an Advanced party of seven officers and 30 other ranks to India within a month, to attend a Jungle Training Course in the Nilgiri Hills near Madras; and thirdly, to release to Civilian Life in a few weeks time the earliest groups conscripted in World War II, who would be replaced by the latest batch of enlisted National Servicemen. Although initially the latter order did not affect greatly the Regiment's officer strength, it did remove many of the experienced sergeants and corporals. Thus the regiment was faced with the task of restructuring its sub units, team building and starting to train for jungle fighting on a Salisbury plain devoid of any thick trees – for which purpose the officers attended many a JEWT (Jungle Exercise Without Trees).

In early July the training cadre left by sea for India in company with parties from the other major units of the 6th Airborne Division, arriving at their jungle school shortly before VJ Day (15th August 1945) where they remained for some days, and unenthusiastically, undergoing jungle training. The rest of the regiment spent the summer carrying out individual jungle drills and by sending companies off to various UK forests for 'jungle sub-unit training'.

DEPLOYMENT TO PALESTINE

Shortly after VJ Day, the Division was informed that it would 'now' be leaving for Palestine to help maintain the peace there, as trouble was brewing between the majority Arab population and the smaller Jewish element – the latter being enlarged weekly by the entry of illegal Jewish immigrants, initially from via the Balkan States. Under a Mandate from the League of Nations after the end of World War I, the UK became the administrative power for Palestine, which covered the area of land from the Lebanon-Syrian borders in the north, along the river Jordan to the east and the border with Egypt to the south. The UK had given pledges, pre-war, that parts of Palestine could, one day, provide a 'Jewish homeland', and that an annual quota of Jewish immigrants would be permitted to enter the Mandated Territory. The Civil Administration, headed by a military High Commissioner, was British-led with a mainly mixed British and Arab staff. The judiciary came from the UK Colonial Office, while the police force was British led with mainly Arab constables. In the area, there was also the British led Arab Legion and the British-officered Trans-Jordan Frontier Force. There was also, prior to VJ Day, a British army presence, whose main teeth arm in late 1945 was an Indian Army Division.

The internal trouble after VJ Day was between the Arabs and the growing Jewish population, and it was inflamed by the increasing numbers of illegal Jewish immigrants who were acquiring additional land that had previously been Arab-owned. The Palestine Police were finding it increasing difficult to control the situation, among other reasons because of a lack of intelligence sources in the Jewish areas. For their part, the Jewish population had been building up a dormant underground 'home guard' known as *Hagana,* and a more militant group called The *Irgun,* which gradually became dominated by the Stern Gang, organised and manned by Jewish ex-servicemen who had served in World War II. Thus, by September 1945, the British authorities were faced with a situation last encountered in Southern Ireland in 1919.

To help restore order, Palestine Command was reinforced by the arrival from October 1945 of the 6th Airborne Division and the 3rd Infantry Division - both had been training since VE Day for the jungle. The British army for seven years had given little thought or training to the maintenance of civil order and were not issued with any specialised equipment for it. In late 1945, officers and their soldiers had to find their own methods of dealing with civilian disorder, which started with crowd riots but spread quickly to acts of sabotage, kidnapping and murder. At the same time soldiers, particularly sentries, had to learn discretion over the use of fire, keeping always in mind the fear that the use of 'undue' force might lead to their appearance 'in the dock' of a military or civil court. Strict training in fire control discipline was therefore all important.

On arrival in Palestine in late October 1945, the Regiment was concentrated with the rest of the 6th Airborne Division in the Gaza area. No. 6 Air Landing Brigade comprised the Regiment, its wartime 'buddies' the 1st Battalion Royal Ulster Rifles and the Argyll & Sutherland Highlanders. Initially the Battalion was housed in a ghastly tented camp at Ras El Ein, where they drew up their allotted scale of vehicles, weapons, ammunition and equipment. A few days later they were moved to a drier tented camp with some huts, called 'Camp 22' at Nathanya – sited in open country near the sea and off the main road and railway line between Gaza, Tel Aviv and Haifa. There they were joined by their Indian Advance Party and remained until April 1946.

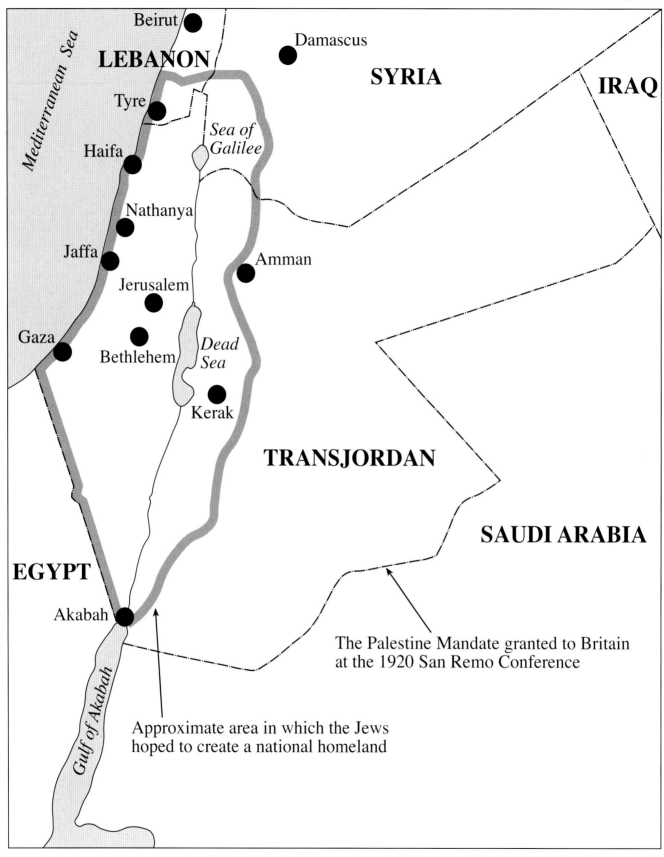

Sketch map of Palestine, 1946.

The author, Colonel P. E. Gerahty, at the time of the Jewish revolt.

Oxfordshire & Buckinghamshire Light Infantry Museum archives

ACTIVITIES IN THE PERIOD JANUARY TO APRIL 1946

Sadly, only a few days after arrival, Colonel Darell-Brown DSO, the Regiment's wartime commander, was badly injured in a jeep crash and evacuated to the UK. Lt Col H. H.van Straubenzee DSO was sent out to assume command from the second-in-command, Major Harry Styles, at the end of January. For the first weeks of the Regiment's stay in Camp 22 the local security situation was quiet. This gave companies the chance to learn the area and to do some internal security (IS) training – although at least one rifle company each day was engaged on static guards, either at the camp or at nearby vulnerable points (VPs), while an immediate readiness platoon was maintained to deal with any incidents which might occur.

At this stage the Regiment boasted eleven officers who were pre-war regulars or had been given regular commissions during the war, and some fifty Regular other ranks – the warrant officers and mostly Sergeant's Mess members dating back from pre-war. The rest of the 700 members of the Battalion were either conscripts from the final two years of the war or post-war young National Servicemen. It was perhaps fortunate that the first weeks in Camp 22 were peaceful enough to allow the Regiment to 'gel'.

The spell was broken in February when Major John Tillett's, 'D' Company, on detachment some miles away, was attacked by terrorists. An immediate platoon counter-attack scared off the opposition without inflicting known casualties. Several subsequent battalion searches of nearby Jewish settlements proved negative, but terrorist mining of the roads and railways started to intensify. This involved the Regiment in constant patrolling and the establishment of snap roadblocks both in retaliation and deterrence. At one stage the Regiment was reinforced by forty Danish Army soldiers who boasted only three surnames between them which caused difficulties in 'C' Company who acquired them. However they proved excellent runners, boxers and diggers (very useful for digging latrines whilst effecting a Cordon and Search operation).

In this period the Regiment was able was able to take full advantage of the camp's playing fields and the nearby rifle range. The Brigade's 3-inch mortar competition was won and the Regimental running team of fifteen runners took part in Palestine Command's Tripoli (near Tyre) to Beirut (Lebanon) road relay race, each runner did up to five miles, and came 4th (the first British team). The first three teams were from the Indian Army, some of whom

Another view of Peter Gerahty, then a captain.
Oxfordshire & Buckinghamshire Light Infantry Museum archives

ran with bags of sugar in their mouths – a trick which some Regimental runners tried later but with disastrous results! Service wives and families were not allowed in Palestine. At this stage, off duty soldiers were permitted to visit Nathanya Town and even parts of Tel Aviv – provided they were in pairs and carrying personal weapons. The problem was transport. Recreational visits in parties were laid on for visits to the sea and local entertainments but not into Jewish dominated areas.

MOVE TO JERUSALEM (APRIL TO OCTOBER 1946)

In accordance with the army's wartime policy in the UK, where units were seldom allowed to stay in the same location for more than four months or so each year to prevent any settling down in routine, the Regiment, with the rest of No. 6 Air Landing Brigade, were moved in April to Jerusalem, where they occupied Alamein Camp

406 (another tented and hutted camp) on the road from the city to Bethlehem. Here the Regiment learnt that it was to leave the 6th Airborne Division to become part of 31 Independent Infantry Brigade and to be minus its coveted red berets. A ceremonial parade was held to mark the occasion with Major General A. J. H. J Cassell OBE, DSO, the GOC of 6 Airborne, taking the salute.

In June Lt Col van Straubenzee was posted as GS01 of the 6th Airborne Division and in due course Lt Col 'Firpo' Ward arrived to command – Firpo being a nickname that he had acquired in the 52nd prior to World War II after a popular Indian restaurant he frequented. This was his 3rd Battalion Command.

The change of terrain to an urban setting where the Stern Gang was to be found in numbers, was a challenge. Half the Battalion each day was involved in guard duties, including the provision of a complete company guard

Sergeant Russell, Private Smith and Captain D. H. Arkell.

for security with ten per cent for ceremonial purposes at the High Commissioners' residence and Headquarters (on the British-named 'Hill of Evil Counsel'!) The High Commissioner at that time was Lt General Sir 'Bubbles' Barker, late of the 60th Rifles, and an old 'friend' of the Regiment. The rest of the Battalion would be engaged on foot patrols, provision of a Lightning Platoon and on routine training.

The Regiment's first operation as a Battalion in this phase took place on 17th June when, for the first time, authority was given for the search of the Jewish Agency, which was known to be controlling terrorist activities. The Regiment's task was to place a covert close-cordon around the perimeter, this difficult night manoeuvre being successfully achieved without incident to allow a parachute battalion to enter for the internal search. There was of course much verbal 'Micky taking' by the Regiment of the 'Red Berets' as they passed through! The cordon was in position for ten days, with the Ulsters taking over for 24 hours every other day.

Later, on the Queen's Birthday, a large detachment from the Regiment lined the route for the traditional march past outside the King David Hotel. A number of Battalion Cordon and Search operations were carried out at Jewish Settlements in the area, and at a potash factory on the Dead Sea where arms were found in numbers and wanted suspects detained, who had to be persuaded to

march to the screening area up a steep hill.

On 22st July 1946 the King David Hotel, part of which housed Command HQ was blown up with many casualties (not guarded by the Regiment) and 'D' Company was turned out to cordon it off and to apply a local curfew. Many Regimental officers who were not on duty, afterwards claimed they were just about to enter the hotel for a haircut when the bomb went off! It was the biggest bombing incident since VJ Day.

Thereafter, terrorist activities in the area and elsewhere in the Mandate intensified, with road mining in particular becoming more frequent, and on 30th October Jerusalem Railway Station was blown up (again not under Regimental guard). In between, a platoon from the Regiment had to disperse an Arab mob bent on attacking local Jews in the Old City. In mid-November, the Battalion moved out of the area to Haifa, having had the good fortune not to have sustained a single casualty from terrorist activity. Our only fatal casualty occurred during a non-terrorist inter-Arab shooting incident. But our fellow Brigade members had not been seen so lucky and had suffered several fatalities. During this period the Regiment lost the services of their last Normandy Veteran Servicemen including Majors Sandy Smith MC and Freddie Scott MC, as well as losing, for six weeks leave in the UK, their regular officers and regular soldiers in rotation. But these enforced changes gave the younger officers and NCOs excellent opportunities to replace them.

SPORTING ACHIEVEMENTS IN 1946

Despite the operational commitments the Regiments found time to participate in the Palestine Command inter-unit sporting fixtures. The seven-a-side rugby team, egged on by the Reverend Peter Malins, its Irish International Padre, reached the Final of the Army Cup; the Cricket Team had a full season on the excellent civilian Jerusalem Sports Ground (in a secure zone); the Hockey Team won the Command Competition and had only one loss that season; the Cross County Team were 3rd in both the divisional and command races while the athletic team urged on by their former UK Olympic team captain – Lt Col Ward – won most of the individual Brigade and Divisional events and did well at the Command Team meeting finishing 2nd overall.

Parties also found time to visit the more peaceful northern hills for game shooting weekends. In between major incidents, off-duty soldiers in armed pairs could still visit the Old City on recreation, while the officers enjoyed visits to the Jerusalem Amateur Dramatic Society's Plays whose Leading Lady, Miss Jones, was some 20 years later to become a Regimental Officer's wife.

ATHLIT CAMP NEAR HAIFA
(NOVEMBER 1946 TO JANUARY 1947)

The Regiment moved on 9th November 1946 to a miserably wet and cold tented camp at Athlit, some twelve miles from Haifa, alongside the Jewish Illegal Immigration Clearance Camp. It became responsible for ensuring that the Jewish inmates did not escape their warders and were not let out by terrorist elements from outside. The Regiment now came under the command of the 3rd Infantry Brigade, with the 1st Duke of Cornwall's Light Infantry and 2nd Battalion Sherwood Foresters, in 1st Division. Straight away orders were received to patrol the main railway line which was been regularly blown up. In early December however the Regiment was moved suddenly to Zerqua in Trans-Jordan for a fortnight's training for 'Conventional War'. This involved participation in set-piece Brigade training exercises. The Regiment took this change of routine with enthusiasm and satisfied the Brigade Staff. It returned to Athlit on 23rd December 1946 and celebrated Christmas in traditional manner in between its operational duties.

There was a 'blip' in the arrival of sufficient national service replacements and 'A' Company was put into suspended animation. However the 52nd Band arrived for a few months' stay and earned its keep by a full programme of concerts as well as by reinforcing our

A timeless scene in old Jerusalem, but a place of potential danger for servicemen – on 1st July 1946 it was ordered that 'all ranks to be armed when out of camp and to be in groups of not less than four'.

Oxfordshire & Buckinghamshire Light Infantry Museum archives

Further views of the ancient streets and alleyways of Old Jerusalem – picturesque scenes which had changed little since Biblical times, although murderers and terrorists could be lurking around any corner.

Oxfordshire & Buckinghamshire Light Infantry Museum archives

various sports teams. A Royal Guard of Honour was provided by 100 men and the Regimental Band, under the command of Captain P. E. Gerahty, on the occasion of King Abdullah of Trans-Jordon leaving Haifa docks to pay a state visit to Turkey. This took place just after the whole Regiment had been ordered to Haifa to carry out a search of a suburb following the blowing up of the main Police Station. Some 870 adults were screened by the Regiment and ten suspects detained. On 18th January 1947 the Regiment was delighted to be moved back to Camp 22 near Nathanya which it had left a year or so before. Whilst at Athlit, the Regiment paid little direct part with dealing with the illegal immigrants, although some patrols along the shore did take place. Organised off-duty visits to local entertainment centres were still permitted, but all ranks could only go outside the camp in a minimum of four.

CAMP 22 NEAR NATHANYA (JANUARY TO MAY 1947)
Camp 22 had been unoccupied for six months, so the first task was to sanitize it and make it tolerable. To start with the local Internal Security situation was quiet, and sub unit training restarted. However, on 23rd January 1947, a convicted terrorist was hanged and, as a precaution, a third of the Regiment was required to sleep clothed and armed, with vehicle movements permitted only in pairs

with at least two armed guards aboard each vehicle. Jewish retaliation started on the 26th, with the capture of a prominent British official in Jerusalem. At 10 pm that night, the Regiment was ordered to make a dawn search of the Measharim Quarter of Jerusalem, some 60 miles away. The RV took place on time, but the subsequent search proved fruitless and the Regiment returned to Camp 22 that night. Following the kidnap of a British Judge from his Court, the Regiment was then ordered back to Jerusalem to enforce a curfew, but next day both British hostages were released and the Regiment returned to Nathanya.

The next few weeks were calm, although a rifle company had to patrol beaches near Tel Aviv daily to look for immigrants from an illegal ship, when ever one was located on the high seas. Recreational trips to the seaside etc had to be banned because of extensive road mining, and the only off-duty amusements for the soldiers were the camp cinema and watching brigade and divisional cross-country contests in which the Regiment proved successful. Captain Philip Godsal (whose father and grandfather had both been 52nd officers), took command of 'B' Company after a spell as Adjutant.

On 1st March 1947 the local quiet was broken when the 2nd Sherwood Foresters in a neighbouring camp were attacked by mortar and light machine gun fire, causing two fatalities. The Regiment's sentries overlooking the Foresters camp opened fire on the attackers who were in dead ground to that regiment and forced them to retreat, firing wildly at Camp 22 as they ran. The next few weeks proved hectic while martial law was declared in Tel Aviv. This was applied by the rest of the Brigade whilst the Regiment took over all the Brigade static duties. However the Regiment did a Search and Cordon operation on a nearby Jewish settlement, detaining 14 wanted suspects, whilst nightly fighting patrols were sent out to dominate our sector. On 17th March 1947 another search operation proved fruitless. Then on 19th March the Regiment was suddenly told officially that it was to be put into suspended animation, together with all other regiments 2nd Battalions, at some future date. Morale shattering news out of the blue!

Our system of dominating the Regimental sector by nightly fighting patrols was recognised as a success and was recommended by Headquarters Palestine Command for universal adoption. During this time one rifle platoon was detached for duty as Lorried Infantry with 4/7 Royal Dragoon Guards, and were commended by the divisional commander for their good fire discipline. It is of interest to note that during the two battalion searches mentioned above, the Regimental band was used to play martial music near the 'screening cages' to the delight of the small children and everyone else since it made boring searches more interesting for all. It is not known if this use of a military band was ever repeated elsewhere and, sadly, the 52nd Band's tour of duty in Palestine ended shortly afterwards.

For the first half of April 1947, the situation quietened down and some 100 men per day were needed for static duties. However, in mid-month, the terrorists attacked the Field Dressing Station at Nathanya, killing the unarmed guard, and attacked the Divisional Training School and the Convalescent Depot Cinema. Another batch of illegal immigrant ships also appeared off the coast requiring a company to remain on beach patrol. A second rifle company was required to provide night patrols in the woods and on the tracks surrounding Nathanya, whilst everyone else provided the usual static guards. At this stage the Regiment's effective strength was some 550 all ranks. However Regimental morale remained high, and there was no time to ponder on the dismal prospect of suspended animation.

At this time the Regiment suffered its only casualties from terrorists in its whole stay in Palestine when a 15 cwt truck was blown up by a mine and its occupants fired on at close range by terrorists armed with automatic weapons. Fortunately the terrorists detonated their bomb too early and their subsequent aim was so poor that the three regimental soldiers in the vehicle were only slightly wounded and returned to Camp 22 a few days later. In early May, Lt Col Ward left to command and form the Regiment's 4th (or TA) Battalion, his replacement being Lt Col Styles, the former 2nd-in-Command, who was to join the Regiment from the UK. The current Regimental 2nd-in-Command, Major Charles Mason, became acting Commanding Officer for the interim. On 15th May 1947 the Regiment was ordered to Jerusalem to become

Members of the Regiment pose by a jeep and a Bren Gun Carrier while on patrol in Jerusalem.
Oxfordshire & Buckinghamshire Light Infantry Museum archives

The blowing up of the King David Hotel, the British headquarters in Palestine, on 22nd July 1946. This incident, which resulted in the deaths of 92 people including 41 Arabs, 28 Britons and 17 Jews, was the worst atrocity carried out by Jewish terrorists during the period of the British Mandate.

under command of 8 Independent Infantry Brigade with the Argyll & Sutherland Highlanders, 2nd Sherwood Foresters and 1st Royal Hampshire Regiment.

SECOND TOUR IN JERUSALEM
(15TH MAY TO 1ST AUGUST 1947)

During this tour the Regiment was required to live in two separate locations: Battalion HQ with 'B' and 'C' Companies in one building - 'The Hospice De la Notre Dame' in C Zone, situated outside one of the main gates to the Old City, while 'D' and 'S' Companies were in the RAPC Camp at the 'Syrian Orphanage' in the notorious terrorist Measharim Quarter in D Zone, under the command of Major Peter Everett. A & B Zones of Jerusalem became the responsibility of the rest of the Brigade. Neither regimental building was easy to defend or comfortable to live in. At the Hospice for example, two or even three soldiers had to occupy cells built for one. In consequence, sentry posts had to be changed constantly to deter would-be attackers, which meant constant re-typing of orders for sentries and patrols. These measures appear to have worked, as neither building was attacked during our two and a half month occupation.

The Regiment's duties in Jerusalem consisted in providing guards in our two zones on Police HQ and on Barclays Bank; of manning road blocks; running a 'pass' office; of carrying out daily snap checks and of providing three mobile 'Lightning Platoons' at immediate notice in the event of an incident. These tasks required the employment of nine officers, 52 NCO's, and 236 soldiers nightly – out of a total strength of some 550 all ranks.

Lack of sleep soon became a general problem! The prize job was to be a member of a 'Lightning Platoon' with its opportunity for initiative and offensive action in getting to and dealing with an incident within minutes.

The most successful action was by a platoon of 'D' Company, commanded by Lieutenant John Thome (son of a regimental commander and himself to become an eminent amateur jockey who finished second on his own horse in the Grand National Steeplechase). His platoon task was to search for three armed men who had raided a bank. This was unsuccessful, but the platoon did discover a large arms cache in a slum area. Another platoon on its way to an incident from the Syrian Orphanage had a White armoured scout car damaged by a prematurely detonated mine, fortunately with no casualties to its occupants, whilst on its way to help another unit's vehicle which had been badly damaged by another mine.

On top of its routine duties, the Regiment was called upon to provide men, at that time not on another duty, to help in impromptu searches for arms caches on waste ground. For the first time these searches were aided by mine dogs and mine detectors, covered by British 'spotter aircraft'. By July 1947 Jerusalem was in the forefront of the growing terrorist activity throughout the Mandate. Three or four incidents would occur daily with the general alarm sounded. When it did, the whole Regiment was required to stand to at action stations at all their many posts and it was a fact that no installation guarded by the Regiment was ever attacked. Between 20-24 July, two large-scale fire fights with terrorists developed near the Syrian Orphanage, and the city rang with mortar bomb explosions and the crack of fire, while the night was illuminated with tracer bullets and Verey Light cartridges.

Most of the noise and danger outside the immediate vicinity of the engagement came from trigger-happy Arab constables on rooftops, putting up what they thought was defensive fire, but frightening our Lightning Platoons called to cordon the area much more than any terrorists who might or might not have been present. In the middle of the month, and amid the deteriorating internal security situation, with the police and other units in the Brigade suffering daily casualties, the Regiment had been informed, out of the blue, that it was to hand over its operational duties in Jerusalem by 31st July and was to be replaced by the 1st Battalion Irish Guards. It was then to move to the Gaza Area for immediate disbandment. Shattering news, but the Regiment was too busy just then to worry about its implications. The changeover was successfully carried out, but two Irish Guardsmen became casualties from a mine detonation almost immediately after their arrival.

THE FINAL CHAPTER
(1ST AUGUST TO 15TH NOVEMBER 1947)

The road movement to Jerusalem to camp 'C', Khassa, some ten miles north of Gaza, was successfully executed on 1st August 1947 but, sadly, the Cook-Sergeant (Comes) was killed in a traffic accident en-route (a fate that had sadly befallen several other regimental soldiers earlier in the campaign). Camp 'C' was a wired-in area of desert that had been properly looked after and had been left in a spotless condition. An ironic situation, considering the Regiment's previous camp problems, especially as it was told it was to move to Egypt within three weeks and was required to strike camp and to strip it before it left! On 2nd August the Regiment was ordered to despatch 160 men to Greece, mainly from 'B' and 'C' companies, in 72 hours' time. This was followed by the despatch of two officers and another 112 other ranks on 13th August to join the 1st Duke of Cornwall's Light Infantry in Cyprus, to be followed by acting RSM Stevenson DCM and 18 other ranks to 7 Para on 20th August – moves which involved the Adjutant and Orderly Room staff in much burning of the midnight oil in producing the necessary documentation.

Meanwhile the Quartermaster, Lieutenant W. S. Stuart and his staff, worked flat-out to hand back to a camp in Haifa (100 miles away) all the battalion's stores, ammunition, equipment and transport (less personal weapons): all had to be checked, counter-checked and signed-for, loaded, unloaded, guarded and escorted by armed men from an ever diminishing number of regimental soldiers left to provide the essential manpower. This tight schedule was not helped by inevitable timing failures by Royal Army Service Corps Transport and by terrorist mining activities. Special farewell dinners were held before each major draft left, with a final dinner for the remnants – with a local band engaged to play popular music – taking place two days before the camp was closed. The officers were meanwhile entertained by

A scene over the edge of Jerusalem.   *Oxfordshire & Buckinghamshire Light Infantry Museum archives*

A scene of bustle and activity at the port of Haifa.   *Oxfordshire & Buckinghamshire Light Infantry Museum archives*

their Peninsular War colleagues in Chestnut Troop of the 1st Royal Horse Artillery, who were stationed nearby.

On 22nd August 1947 the rump of the Regiment left Palestine for Egypt on schedule with the doubtful honour of being the Infantry Battalion in that unhappy country with the longest period of continuous active service and having suffered, so it was believed, fewer 'battle' casualties, than any other unit of similar size. One wonders whether any other Regular Army Regiment has ever been broken up and scattered to the winds, whilst on active service, in such a short space of time and with so little public attention. Of course the press of that era were not interested and there were no wives and family living in a close community to attract publicity. As the *Regimental Chronicle* for 1947 declared, 'All ranks in the Regiment tried to do their duty in Palestine impartially and with justice and tried to live up to the highest tradition of the Regiment during its 191-year history'.

REFLECTIONS IN RETROSPECT

In its 20 months of active service in Palestine, in addition to its daily toll of Internal Security deterrent duties and more offensive operations at company or platoon level, its regimental HQ had taken to the field to command and control some 15 battalion-sized operations lasting a day or longer. It is of interest to note that, apart from receipt of the Palestine Clasp to the General Service Medal which was received by all soldiers who served in that country for the minimum period, no officers and no soldiers of the Regiment received any award in recognition of their

outstanding service in that long-drawn out contest. Other Regiments and Corps were no doubt treated similarly. It was a campaign during which the last few groups of wartime national servicemen of all ranks, and their successors who joined after VJ Day, bore the brunt of the workload and of any dangers that were involved - and a very good job they made of it, especially the young officers and the NCOs who displayed enthusiasm and initiative. Most of these men especially, and those in the combat arms, would probably admit now that they were better men for the experience.

THE REGIMENT'S FINAL WEEKS

On arrival in Suez the Regiment, now down to some 200 all ranks, was housed in the comfortable Base Transit Depot. With the sea adjacent and no Internal Security restrictions in force, all ranks were able to make use of the local entertainment facilities and of shops full of goods which were still alleged to be unobtainable in the UK. Further small drafts were dispatched to local units until finally the Regiment now six officers, two WO2s, and 88 other ranks strong, embarked for the UK on *HMT Clan Lament* (a converted cargo vessel of some 10,000 tons), together with the 1st Royal West Kents and 2nd Royal Ulster Rifles, both at full strength.

The official Regimental Rear Party was Lt Col Styles in command, Major C. Mason 2nd-in-Command, Captain P. E. Gerahty (Adjutant) Lieutenant W. S. Stuart QM, Lieutenants P. Jordan and E. A. R. Partridge (Colour Party) and 15 regular other ranks who included Lane Corporal

Purkins (who had joined the 52nd in India in 1922). Another sixty-five national servicemen who were due for discharge in the UK were added to the Rear Party.

The *Clan Lament* docked at Liverpool on 12th September 1947, and the Regimental party entrained for Oxford to be met there that afternoon by General Sir Bernard Paget - the Colonel of the Regiment - and a group of distinguished Regimental Officers and local dignitaries. The 52nd Rear Party was housed in the Cowley Barracks Regimental Depot, with the 52nd flag flying appropriately from its last HQ - the cricket pavilion. The Colours were hung in the Officers Mess, Regimental property was placed in the Museum and the strength was whittled down during the next month to a final cadre of Captain P. E. Gerahty, the ORQMS and two NCOs.

The 52nd officially ceased to exist on 15th November 1947 when its flag was hauled down jointly by this trio and the last Part II Order was issued. Thus, 'a Regiment unsurpassed in Arms since Arms were born of Man' (to quote its best known Historian – Sir Arthur Bryant), departed from the Army List into suspended animation! This was subsequently changed, some months later, by the Army Board at the request of the Regimental Committee, to official amalgamation with the 43rd Light Infantry to create the 1st Battalion the Oxfordshire & Buckinghamshire Light Infantry (43rd & 52nd).

The names of all the officers known to have served in the 52nd between 3rd September 1939 and 15th November 1947 were inscribed on a large silver salver which was, for many years, kept in the Regimental Museum. This silver salver was bought using Mess money, following a decision reached at the last official 52nd Officers Mess Meeting.

This article was written by Colonel (Ret) P. E. Gerahty CBE in June 2008 (in his 87th year), from memory and from the contents of the *Regimental Chronicles* for 1946 and 1947. In the period covered by this article he held the following appointments in the 52nd light Infantry;

July-November 1945 - OIC Regimental Training Cadre/ Advance Party in India.

December 1945 to January 1947 - 2IC (and for periods OC) Letter 'C' Company;

25th January to 15 November 1947 - Adjutant.

A General Service Medal with Palestine clasp awarded to Lieutenant A. J. R. Steele. The medal has a purple ribbon with central green stripe.
Oxfordshire & Buckinghamshire Light Infantry Museum

Jewish Civilians relax in the sunshine at Tel Aviv. It was impossible for the army and police to identify the terrorists, who simply melted into the crowd. *Oxfordshire & Buckinghamshire Light Infantry Museum archives*

SOME NOTES ON THE HOME GUARD
In OXFORDSHIRE & BUCKINGHAMSHIRE
Stanley C. Jenkins MA

Less than twenty years after the end of World War I, the United Kingdom was plunged into World War II - the declaration of war against Nazi Germany being broadcast live on the BBC by Prime Minister Neville Chamberlain at lunchtime on Sunday 3rd September 1939. With horrific memories of the 1914-18 conflict still fresh in many minds, many people expected that the United Kingdom would soon be devastated by fleets of massed Nazi bombers. Nervous individuals were hardly reassured when, shortly after the declaration of war, air raid sirens wailed out across many parts of the country – though in reality this initial scare was merely a false alarm.

Spurred on by the worrying events in Europe, large numbers of men volunteered for service in the armed forces, and had to be hastily trained and kitted out. In August, at the end of the last peace-time Annual Camp, the key parties of the territorial battalions of the Oxfordshire & Buckinghamshire Light Infantry were ordered to report to drill halls to prepare for mobilisation, and on the day that war broke out the Territorial Army was embodied.

THE RETREAT FROM DUNKIRK

The first few months of the war in the west were so uneventful that people spoke derisively of 'The Phoney War', although military activity was taking place in far away places such as Norway or the South Atlantic. One of the first Oxfordshire casualties was Able Seaman Kenneth Billett of Witney, who was killed on 8th April 1940 when his destroyer. *HMS Glowworm*, attacked a German heavy cruiser.

The German Army attacked on 10th May 1940, and the 'British Expeditionary Force' was soon obliged to withdraw across Belgium to the line of the River Escaut – where three Oxfordshire & Buckinghamshire Light Infantry battalions were engaged in defensive actions to the south of Tournai. Desperate rearguard actions enabled the bulk of the British Expeditionary Force to reach the comparative safety of Dunkirk where, by Monday 27th May 1940, 115 acres of docks and five miles of quays had been destroyed by German bombing, while the acrid black smoke from two million tons of blazing fuel oil towered 11,000 feet into the sky. In the absence of proper port facilities, many thousands of men were being embarked from the open beaches, or from the east and west 'moles' – long, mainly wooden piers that extended seawards for a distance of about 1,400 yards and served as breakwaters.

In the next few days, many thousands of men were rescued from the beleaguered port, and by Tuesday 4th June, 338,226 men had been conveyed across the Channel in a variety of vessels – many members of the Oxfordshire & Buckinghamshire Light Infantry being evacuated aboard the destroyers *HMS Worcester*, *HMS Scimitar* and the 2,384 ton Southern Railway steamer *Maid of Orleans*.

FORMATION OF THE OXFORDSHIRE HOME GUARD

The Fall of France heralded the most serious phase of the war and, in expectation of a Nazi invasion, road signs and station name boards were removed. The regular army was in no state to repel the expected invasion, many of the men who had returned from Dunkirk being totally exhausted, while huge amounts of vital equipment had been destroyed in France to prevent it from falling into enemy hands.

Under these circumstances, Winston Churchill, at that time First Lord of the Admiralty, called for the establishment of an organisation which he called a 'Home Guard', and it was, accordingly, decided that a new volunteer force would be formed for the defence of the British homeland. On 14th May 1940 the Secretary of State for War, Anthony Eden, appealed for able-bodied men aged 17 or over to register for service in a home defence force or local militia to be known as 'The Local Defence Volunteers'. The response was immediate and almost overwhelming as thousands of men enrolled for service in the new force. In July 1940 the LDV, which

Arm bands worn by members of the Witney 'Local Defence Volunteers'. The 'LDV' was re-named The Home Guard in August 1940. *Witney & District Museum WIT98005*

Above: A group photograph showing members of the 3rd Battalion Oxfordshire Home Guard taken in front of St Mary the Virgin Parish Church, Witney.
Below: Members of the Witney Home Guard also in front of St Mary's.   *both Witney & District Museum WIT1445, WIT97008*

now had a strength of 1,472,505, was renamed 'The Home Guard'.

Many of the volunteers were veterans of the Great War, and one former Home Guardsman remembered his first LDV route march which brought back vivid memories of: *'the Menin Road, of loose, shifting, exasperating cobbles, of the smell of cordite and the scream of shrapnel … our first route march was a silent one, with each of us busy with those thoughts of the past, trudging a Berkshire road with that almost automatic one-ness of movement which the old soldier can never lose'.*

The main threat, in the summer of 1940, was perceived to be from enemy parachutists and 'Fifth Columnists', and in this context there were inevitable false alarms, with innocent persons being rounded up and confined in makeshift cells. On the night of 17th-18th September 1940 an invasion was thought to be taking place and, the codeword 'Cromwell' having been given, the Home Guard rang the church bells as a warning of imminent attack. The next few weeks provided 'many exciting and amusing incidents, until the approaching winter made the chances of invasion less probable', and the Home Guard units settled down to a programme of organisation and training.

The Oxfordshire Home Guard was originally commanded by the reassuringly-named Brigadier-General A. Courage, but in November 1940 General Courage retired as Zone Commander, his replacement being Captain the Hon. B. Mitford RN. There were, by this time, seven Oxfordshire Home Guard companies within the county, with headquarters in Banbury, Bicester, Chipping Norton, Bullingdon, Henley, Oxford and Oxford University.

Following the publication of Army Council Instruction 653 in June 1940, these units were subsequently organised into eleven battalions of varying strengths, the largest units, such as the 1st (Banbury) and 2nd (Bicester) battalions, having over 1,500 men and 1,600 men respectively, while the 3rd (Chipping Norton) Battalion ultimately had a strength of 60 officers and 2,191 men. There was also an Anti-Aircraft Battery, while the 6th (Oxford City) Battalion was later asked to form a 'Rocket Battery' at Cowley. Oxfordshire Home Guardsmen were affiliated to the Oxfordshire & Buckinghamshire Light Infantry and, as such, they wore the familiar stringed bugle horn cap badge.

'A GOOD PLACE TO BE IF ANYTHING SHOULD HAPPEN'

Local Home Guard units met in a variety of unlikely premises, including schools, church halls and private houses. Inns were also pressed into use as Home Guard meeting places – for example, the headquarters of the Bullingdon Battalion, which had initially been in Wheatley, was moved to the Swan Hotel at Tetsworth on 26th May 1940.

It might be thought that South Leigh station, on the Great Western Railway branch line between Oxford and Witney, was one of the more unusual Home Guard meeting places although, in reality, several other local stations were also used by the Home Guard – other examples being Wantage Road (then in Berkshire) and High Wycombe. At one stage in the war, South Leigh station was being put to good use by local Home Guard members such as Arthur Smith and Rob Brown, who met there for regular training sessions! Rob Brown remembered that 'it was quite a good headquarters' because it was one of the public few buildings in the village and, moreover, it had a telephone link to the outside world.

There were about eight men in the South Leigh Home Guard sub-section, and they would be 'on call' at the station every night – palliasses being provided in the tiny waiting room for the benefit of men who were not out on patrol in the blacked-out countryside. The railway was, at that time, kept open throughout the night in connection with military traffic, and the station was regarded as 'a good place to be, in case anything should happen'.

HOME GUARD EQUIPMENT

In the early days, members of the Local Defence Volunteers had worn civilian clothes, although the volunteers were issued with simple armbands bearing the initials 'LDV'. Soon, however, the army grudgingly released surplus uniforms, helmets and other equipment from its stores – much of it was too big or too small for the wearers because the standard sizes were held back for the regular forces.

The meagre supply of weapons and equipment available for use by the Home Guard during the early months of 1940 included shotguns, 'Molotov bombs'

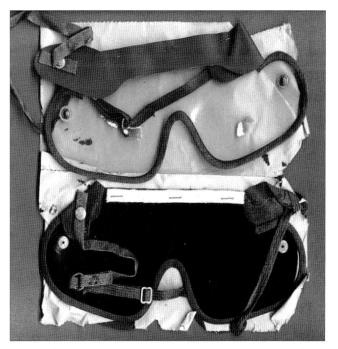

A set of gas protection goggles issued to members of the Witney Home Guard. *Witney & District Museum WIT98003*

and pikes, but these deficiencies were remedied during the following winter and, thereafter, 'matters gradually improved until every man had an up-to-date personal weapon, while examples of every conceivable bomb, grenade, mortar and anti-tank device eventually found their way into the local Home Guard armouries'.

The standard Home Guard weapon was the Ross bolt-action rifle, though Sten guns, Lee-Metfords and other weapons were also employed. Lieutenant-Colonel A.V.Spencer, the Commander of the Bullingdon Battalion, recalled that, by the late summer of 1940, the Home Guard had become a properly-equipped force:

'By the end of August 1940 uniform and equipment was being issued comparatively freely, and each man had a suit of denim, a pair of boots and anklets, while about one-third had great coats, haversacks, belts and steel helmets; blankets and ground sheets also were coming in. The arms on charge at the end of the year were 570 .300 American rifles, 60 Browning automatic rifles, 20 Browning machine guns and 24 Lewis guns. All weapons were .300 bore, with the exception of some .303 Lee-Enfield rifles, obtained from an unofficial source. There were forty rounds SAA per rifle and 550 per machine gun available for operations, with a very small surplus for practice'.

HOME GUARD DUTIES

The function of the Home Guard had been enlarged from observation and reporting to include delay and obstruction of the enemy and the protection of towns and villages. Road blocks were erected at the entrances to villages, at bridges and other tactical points, constructed usually of tree trunks on a pivot with a wheel for easier operation. These were guarded by slit trenches and other fire positions. Defended localities in and around the villages were also constructed. The role of the defenders, however, was still completely static.

Training was carried out, mostly at section level, on Sunday mornings and one or two evenings a week. It must be remembered that Home Guard duties except in the event of active operations were not to interfere with civilian work of national importance in which the majority of all ranks were engaged. At Witney, for example, many members of the Home Guard worked for De Havillands at Witney Aerodrome, so many aircraft workers having volunteered for Home Guard duties that a special 'De Havillands Platoon' was formed. It was only on Sundays and after work hours, therefore, that they were available for duty or training.

A large proportion of the members of the Bullingdon Battalion, as indeed of all battalions in the county except the 6th (Oxford City) Battalion were engaged in agriculture, and their free time especially during hay-making and harvest and in the case of milkers, was very limited. None the less, attendance at parades was very good. Much assistance in training was given by the Regimental Depot, who sent out NCOs to give instruction

to platoons and sections at their own headquarters and also ran short courses of instruction in weapon and other training at Cowley Barracks, to which members of the Home Guard went on Saturday afternoons and Sunday mornings.

LORD LONGFORD & THE HOME GUARD

It is interesting to note that Frank Pakenham, the future Lord Longford, was a member of the Oxfordshire Home Guard. He had enrolled as a private in the (Territorial) Light Infantry in 1939 and, at the outbreak of World War II, he was commissioned as a second lieutenant in The Oxfordshire & Buckinghamshire Light Infantry. Evelyn Waugh recorded meeting him 'in uniform, full of ambitions to serve in any capacity, civil or military, greatly dismayed by the obscenity of conversations among private soldiers'.

Sadly, 2nd Lieutenant Pakenham's career as a soldier was a complete and utter disaster. He was incapable of undertaking routine tasks such as making his bed or keeping his equipment clean, and the psychological strain soon made itself felt. Having suffered a severe personal crisis, this member of a long-established military family was invalided out of the Army on 'medical' grounds in 1940. This was a bitter blow for a man who, despite his very obvious eccentricities, had been determined to combat the rise of fascism, a political creed which he utterly abhorred.

In an attempt, perhaps, to prove that he was, after all, a worthy descendant of Wellington, Frank Pakenham helped Maurice Bowra to raise and command the 'South Company' of the Oxford City Home Guard Battalion. Unfortunately, even this worthwhile activity descended into pure farce when he was shot in the foot by the only member of his company to possess any live ammunition.

OXFORDSHIRE HOME GUARD ORDER OF BATTLE

The Oxfordshire Home Guard ultimately reached a strength of 13,500 men, the various battalions being as follows:

- 1st Oxfordshire (Banbury) Battalion: Lieutenant-Colonel A. Stockton (1940); Lieutenant-Colonel H. T. Lefeaux MC OBE (1940-45). Final strength 60 officers and 1,533 men.
- 2nd Oxfordshire (Bicester) Battalion: Lieutenant-Colonel Lloyd-Mostyn (1940-41). Final strength 54 officers and 1,670 men.
- 3rd Oxfordshire (Chipping Norton) Battalion: Lieutenant-Colonel E. T. Chamberlayne DSO, TD (1940); Lieutenant-Colonel The Hon. B. Mitford DSO (1940-45). Final strength 60 officers and 2,191 men.
- 4th Oxfordshire (Bullingdon) Battalion: Lieutenant-Colonel A. V. Spencer DSO (1940-45). Final strength 58 officers and 1,208 men.
- 5th Oxfordshire (Henley) Battalion: Lieutenant-Colonel H. C. Tweedie DSO, OBE (1940); Lieutenant-Colonel A. F. R. Wiggins (1945). Final strength 57

officers and 1,382 men.

- 6th Oxfordshire (Oxford City) Battalion: Captain E. L. Francis (1940); Lieutenant-Colonel J. A. Douglas (1940-45). Final strength 83 officers and 2,069 men.
- 7th Oxfordshire (Oxford University Senior Training Corps) Battalion: Colonel C. H. Wilkinson MC (1940-45). Final strength 4 officers and 444 cadets.
- Oxford 'D' Company: Major F. Beecher (1942-45). Final strength 8 officers and 244 men.
- 111th (101st Oxfordshire HG):- 'Z' Anti-Aircraft Battery: Major R. B. Freeman MBE (1943-45). Final strength 35 officers and 1,400 men.
- South Midland Home Guard Transport Column: Lieutenant-Colonel W. B. Street (1943-45).

THE BUCKINGHAMSHIRE HOME GUARD

Following the 'wireless' broadcast appeal made on 14th May 1940, many hundreds of Buckinghamshire men registered at police stations for enrolment in the Local Defence Volunteers. The response was truly magnificent, and suitable commanders were soon appointed to set up the necessary organization. On Friday 17th May 1940, Colonel P. A. Hall was appointed commander for Buckinghamshire with the approval of Brigadier MacMullen, the commander of the South Midland Area in which Buckinghamshire was then included.

A conference of county commanders and chief constables was called at Area Headquarters on the following day, and it was agreed that Buckinghamshire would be sub-divided into seven areas, which would correspond to the local police divisions. It was initially envisaged that the new force was would have no formal ranks, and apart from the Area Commanders, all leaders were expected to be selected by merit, election or common consent – the implication being that the Local Defence Volunteers would be a purely local force for the protection of individual towns, villages and hamlets.

The first few months involved an immense amount of work, while the lack of uniforms, arms, equipment and financial backing engendered 'the largest amount of honourable indignation, jealousy and deliberate misappropriation that has possibly ever existed in this county at one time'. Nevertheless, by 'gradual and rather grudging stages' the Buckinghamshire local defence force developed into a pattern very similar to that of the regular army, with commissioned officers, non-commissioned officers and a light framework of discipline, 'all this to the intense delight of many old warriors who had borne with ill-concealed dissatisfaction a state of affairs that they regarded as deplorable'.

The seven areas became seven battalions, each battalion being sub-divided into companies and sections. By July 1940, when this force of enthusiastic part-timers was re-named The Home Guard, it had developed into a conventional military organisation, with 'proper' ranks and uniforms. As in Oxfordshire, it was agreed that the Buckinghamshire Home Guardsmen would be affiliated to the Oxfordshire & Buckinghamshire Light Infantry, the 'swan' badge of the Bucks Battalion being adopted as the cap badge of the Buckinghamshire Home Guard.

As regards routine work and duties, all over the county vast numbers of men were kept up all night manning numerous and overlapping observation posts. Government departments, local Authorities and business leaders called for guards on what were deemed to be vulnerable installations such as aerodromes, factories and railway lines. Indeed, the Home Guard devoted much of their time to patrolling railway installations and, in some places the local railway stations became Home Guard headquarters or assembly points.

As in other counties, the Buckinghamshire Home Guard were called upon to man block-houses and pill-boxes which were, in many instances, erected at 'nodal points' at which ambushes could be staged. Trenches were dug: 'at every conceivable point, frequently sited most unsuitably; and road-blocks, usually in the form of a tree with a wheel at one end, to hold up wheeled traffic, were placed to obstruct vital roads all over the county'. Despite their apparent eccentricities, the Home Guard rapidly became a force to be reckoned with and, as humorists pointed out, sudden challenges and occasional random shots 'soon made the country a land unfit for anyone but heroes to live in, at any rate after dark'.

THE 'HOME GUARD COACH'

At High Wycombe station the Great Western Railway fitted-up an ancient four-wheeled passenger vehicle as a mess room for the Home Guard, the vehicle involved being former composite No. 6615. It was later decided that a dismounted coach body (possibly the same 'Home Guard Coach') would be lifted onto the up platform as accommodation for the Home Guard at an estimated cost of £59. Unfortunately, the final cost was £76 16s. 3d. because 'Sunday labour had to be worked', and 'the engine power and crane hire' was more expensive than had been anticipated!

In addition to providing accommodation for the Home Guard, the High Wycombe railway station also served as the headquarters for a detachment of Air Raid Wardens, who were comfortably installed in the Ladies' Waiting Room on Platform One – this being the source of some tension between the Home Guard and the ARP Wardens because the Ladies Waiting Room had been fully-equipped with cupboards and beds, with a gas ring in the nearby Foreman's Office!

THE 'OSTERLEY REDS' & THE HOME GUARD TRAINING SCHOOL

Churchill's 'Finest Hour' broadcast on 18th June 1940 had paid tribute to the Spanish Republicans who had resisted Fascism during the Spanish Civil War, while at the same time many left-wingers became enthusiastic supporters of the Home Guard, which they regarded as a kind of 'citizen army' on the lines of the Spanish Republican militias that had defended Madrid. In this context, Tom Wintringham (1898-1949) and other veterans of the Spanish Civil War set up a 'Home Guard Training School' at Osterley Park to train the volunteers in the techniques of guerrilla warfare – which was one of the tasks of the Home Guard, as well as the rounding up of enemy parachutists and the much-feared 'fifth columnists'.

Many establishment figures were highly-suspicious of Wintringham and his so-called 'Osterley Reds', who were seen as socialists and communists who could not trusted to lead the Home Guard 'along the paths of truth and righteousness'. Yet, despite a certain amount of official opposition, the school trained over 5,000 men during its first six months of operation, Buckinghamshire Home Guardsmen being among them.

EXPANSION OF THE BUCKINGHAMSHIRE HOME GUARD

As the numbers and strength of the Buckinghamshire Home Guard began to increase, it became necessary to add additional battalions, and in November 1940 the original 6th Battalion was sub-divided into four battalions which then became the 6th, 8th, 9th and 10th Battalions – all covering the southern part of the county. Following a later sub-division, the 5th Battalion was split to form the 5th and 11th Battalions, the 5th being concentrated in the Beaconsfield, Gerrards Cross and Denham area, whereas the 11th Battalion covered Chesham, Amersham and the surrounding districts.

In the north of the county, a further subdivision took place when a new battalion, the 12th, took over parts of the 1st, 2nd and 3rd Battalion areas. Meanwhile, a 13th battalion was formed by employees of the Hawker Aircraft Company at Langley, in the south of the county. Later still, the Buckinghamshire Home Guard acquired a rocket battery at Slough, an Anti-Aircraft battery covering the Windsor area and a Mechanical Transport Company with its headquarters at High Wycombe.

BUCKINGHAMSHIRE HOME GUARD ORDER OF BATTLE

- 1st Battalion: Lieutenant-Colonel H. M. Edwards OBE (1940-45).
- 2nd Battalion: Lieutenant-Colonel Sir Everard Duncombe Bt, DSO, DL (1940-42); Lieutenant-Colonel R. E. Hagley OBE (1942-45).
- 3rd Battalion: Lieutenant-Colonel R. Haworth DSO, MVO (1940-42); Lieutenant-Colonel A. E. Impey (1942-45).
- 4th Battalion: Lieutenant-Colonel H. Beaumont OBE (1940-42); Lieutenant-Colonel L. W. Kentish, D.S.O (1942-45)
- 5th Battalion: Lieutenant-Colonel P. M. Beachcroft OBE (1940-41; Lieutenant-Colonel W. Gibson, DSO OBE, MC (1941-45).
- 6th Battalion: Colonel S. W .L. Ashwanden. DSO, TD, DL ADC 1940-43. (Disbanded 1943).

- 7th Battalion: Colonel L. L. C. Reynolds DSO, TD, DL (1940-42); Lieutenant-Colonel L. W. Strong (1942-45).
- 8th Battalion: Colonel L. M. Wilson CMG, DSO (1940-42); Lieutenant-Colonel T. L. Wakley (1942-45).
- 9th Battalion: Lieutenant-Colonel W. H. Lewis, DSO, MC (1940-42); Lieutenant-Colonel E. R. Clarke MC (1942-45).
- 10th Battalion: Lieutenant-Colonel H. R. Douglas Harding (1940-42); Major-General Sir Richard Howard-Vyse KCMG, DSO (1942); Lieutenant-Colonel W. R. Corfield MC (1942-45).
- 11th Battalion: Lieutenant-Colonel G. S. Marston DSO, MC (1942-45).
- 12th Battalion: Brigadier-General J. Micklem DSO, MC (1942-45).
- 13th Battalion: Lieutenant-Colonel P. W. S. Bulman CBE, MC, AFC, (1943-45).
- 101st (Bucks Home Guard) Rocket Anti-Aircraft Battery: Major F. S. Low MC (1942-43); Major G.S.Deakin OBE (1943-45).
- 71st (Bucks and Berks) Heavy Anti-Aircraft Battery: Major J. B .S. Bourne-May (1942-45).
- 2003rd (Bucks Home Guard) Mechanical Transport Company: Major E. A. Hearne (1943-44); Major F. W. Tillion (1944-45).

THE END OF THE HOME GUARD

In November 1944 it was announced that The Home Guard was to be officially 'stood down', after four-and-a-half years of continuous activity, as all risk of invasion and incursion had finally disappeared. By that time, members of the Home Guard had won two George Crosses and 13 George Medals, while 1,206 members had been killed on active service, and a further 557 had been seriously injured.

A Home Guard lapel badge worn by a member of the Witney Home Guard. *Witney & District Museum WIT98004*